The Rebeats Cymbal Book

by Rob Cook

ADVANCE DRAFT EDITION

ISBN 978-1-888408-65-2

ADVANCE DRAFT 1.0

Copyright © 2025, Rebeats
P.O. Box 6, Alma, Michgan 48801
All rights for publication and distribution are reerved. No part of this book may be reproduced in any form or by any electronic or mechanical means including information storage and retrieval systems without publisher's written consent.

TABLE OF CONTENTS

TBA

CYMBAL HISTORY

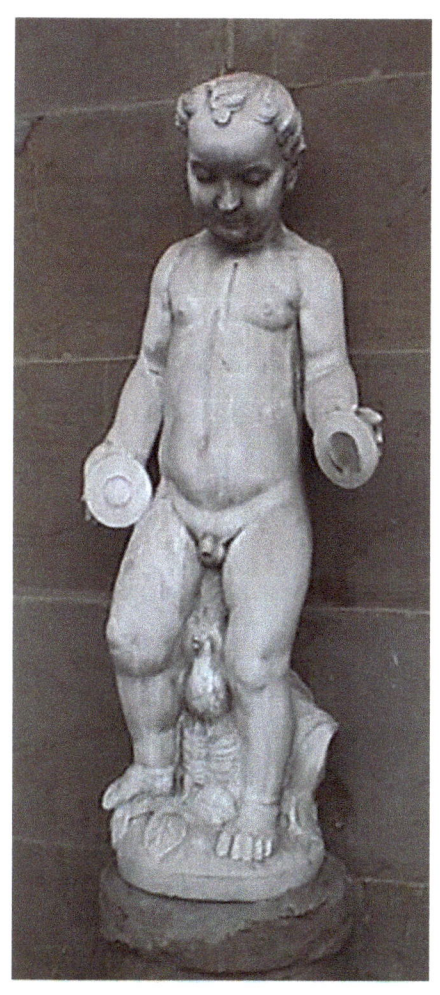

Cymbals as we know them today have evolved over the last few hundred years. Their origins, however, go back thousands of years. Pretty much as soon as bronze was discovered, humans delighted in the resonance of this alloy. The world's museums are well stocked with early bronze "cymbals".

For thousands of years, the most common incarnation of cymbals was a small cup style, often chained together. The sculpture at left used to stand outside a building in Florence near the train station and was a working fountain with water squirting from the penis. I always referred to him as the "pee boy cymbal player."

This QR code will take you to early cymbals at the British Museum in London.

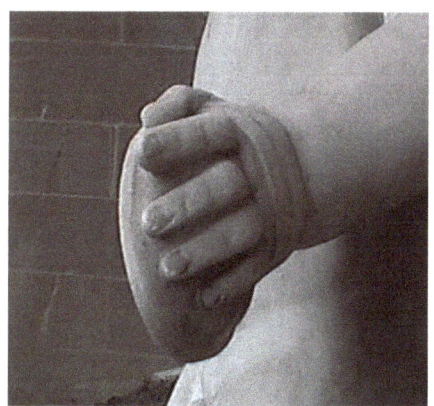

Cymbali di Santa Croce (1659)
By the 1600s, cymbals began to evolve into the style of instruments we know today. This happened not just in Turkey, as evidenced by these Italian cymbals.

CYMBAL BRONZE

Most "Turkish type" bronze cymbals are made of an alloy of about 80% Copper and 20% Tin, often with traces of other elements such as Silver.
This 80/20 alloy is often referred to as B20.
The late artisan cymbalsmith Mike Skiba described the alloy this way:

Cast bronze is a mixed metal, an alloy...NOT an elemental metal. When these elemental metals are mixed with others to form alloys, they must coexist with the physical properties of the other constituent metal(s) and are forced to "get along". Some elemental metals "play well with others" better, while some do not. It just so happens that Copper mixed with Tin results in an alloy that is sonorous (musically appealing) but this is a marriage that requires constant work to remain happy. In an effort to refrain from the minutiae of crystal shape and micron particle size, let's just say that these two elements are quite different from each other...they each bring to the table positive qualities that combine to form a strong partnership, but they have their differences at the same time. Each element has its own natural grain shape and size, but this is where the trouble in the marriage begins...when mixed together under extreme heat they must form a granular bond.

In the case of cymbals, this bond will be tested repeatedly through many more subsequent heat phases, of which the ultimate occurs when the material is forced through rollers to form flat compressed discs. This rolling process pushes the alloy's bonding capability to the limit such that the outer edge of the material almost always splits to some degree. The multi-directional orientation of numerous passes through the rollers forces the material to constantly re-align its bonds. This operation is carried out with the material under extreme heat, but at the same the rollers are cooled by water. To say the least, the marriage of Copper and Tin is severely tested, as they remain locked together. Another partial heating operation follows when the bell is pressed, and this is the first application of true tension under heat, pulling on the center of the disc to raise the material like a miniature cymbal within a field of free metal.

The metal disc at this stage is very brittle and would shatter if hammered. It must be heated and cooled which *"locks the grains in a softer state"*. **There are increasing numbers of cymbal smiths who begin their work with "blanks," the discs that are at this stage. (They do not participate in the casting process.) The blanks are still far from usable cymbals, but they do have a certain amount of internal tension, the property which enables the cymbal to ring in a musical manner. The hammering and lathing processes basically adjust that tension.**

History of the cymbal marketplace in America

Cymbal manufacturing in the United States is generally thought of in terms of *Turkish* cymbal manufacturing. And Turkish cymbal manufacturing in the United States for most of the 20th century was thought of in terms of the Zildjian brand of Turkish cymbals. Before we consider some various aspects of American manufacturing and distribution of Zildjian cymbals, however, I would like to call attention to some lesser known aspects of cymbal history.

American newspapers of the 1800s as far back as the 1860s advertise Turkish, German, and American cymbals. We have a pretty good idea of how the Turkish cymbals were made and what they looked and sounded like.

German Cymbals Of The 1800s

Asked to comment on the German cymbals of the 1800s, German drum historian Fritz Steger tells us: "Most musical instruments for Europe came from the core of the towns of Markneukirchen, Erlbach, Klingenthal, and Schoneck. This area was called Musikwinkel and at the turn of the 20th century produced significant world market share. From 1893 to 1916 there was a US consular agency in Markneukirchen. This became the wealthiest part of Germany, though it was not so much the musical manufacturers who became wealthy as the dealers, the so-called "forwarders". (The "forwarders", of course, included the German-American family Gretsch.) German cymbal makers had access to many sheet metals. German gongs and bronze cymbals were made from 78% copper and 22% tin according to Otto Lueger, writing in 1910. By far the largest numbers of German cymbals produced in the 1800s were brass and nickel silver/German siler/white copper. According to Steger, most of the German catalogs from around 1900 listed cymbals that were hammered, not spun. This was presumably because the production numbers were too small to warrant machine investment, especially since labor was so cheap and the hammered cymbals sounded better.

An American Manufacturer Producing 400 Gongs and 1000 Cymbals Annually in 1876

Union Record, Union, Missouri April 20, 1876

An easier to read transcription of the 1876 clipping:

The only manufactory of gongs and cymbals in this country is in Boston.

From 300 to 400 gongs and 500 pairs of cymbals per year are produced, the price depending upon the size- cymbals of 12 and 14 inches diameter ranging from $24 to $36, and gongs selling at fifty cents per inch in diameter.

clipping courtesy of Jerry Reiman

The Boston "manufactory of cymbals and gongs" referred to in the 1876 newspaper clipping was a company known at that time as Richardson & Lehnert, #13 Bowker Street, Boston.

Carl Lehnert and his brother Henry were listed as musical instrument manufacturers in the Boston directories as early as 1861. Carl formed a partnership with B.F. Richardson and in 1865, their "fine tuned cymbals" were entered in the 10th Exhibition of the Massachusetts Charitable Mechanic Association where they received an award.. Henry Lehnert moved to Philadelphia in 1867 and manufactured brass instruments there. He was best known for his wind instruments, though he did register a patent for a snare drum in 1888 and presumably made cymbals there as well.

Both Carl Lehnert and B.F. Richardson continued to manufacture cymbals and brass wind instruments after their partnership ended by 1878; Benjamin Franklin Richardson was listed as a manufacturer of cymbals and gongs in an 1878 Boston city directory. Carl Lehnert remained at the Bowker Street address and was in 1880 listed as a gong maker.

For master brass workers, it was a simple matter to spin brass discs (they were not cast) into the shape of cymbals. These instruments did not sound as good as cast bronze cymbals, but they did meet the musical demands of the day.

There can be no doubt that Henry Lehnert was serious about percussion instruments. The 1888 patent shown below is for a snare drum with snares on both the top and bottom heads. This concept would be applied by the Ludwig company several decades later. It is not clear from the patent verbiage whether the shell and counterhoops are wood or brass, but Lehnert's businesses were known for their brass instruments, so this is presumably a brass drum.

H. G. LEHNERT.
DRUM.
No. 382,045. Patented May 1, 1888.

TOP SNARES   **BOTTOM SNARES**

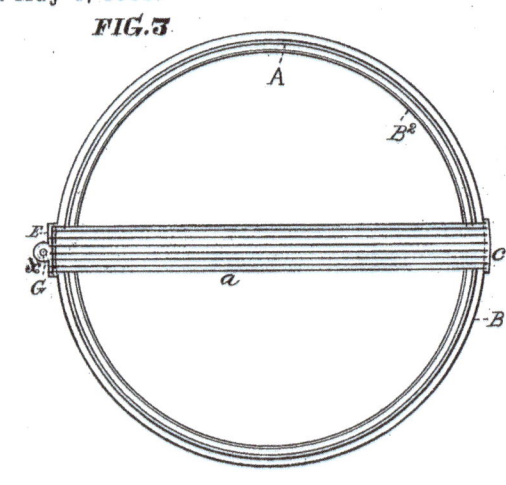

Some examples of Lehnert horns made in the late 1800s

The photos below appear courtesy of historian and collector Robb Stewart

https://www.robbstewart.com/lehnert-instruments

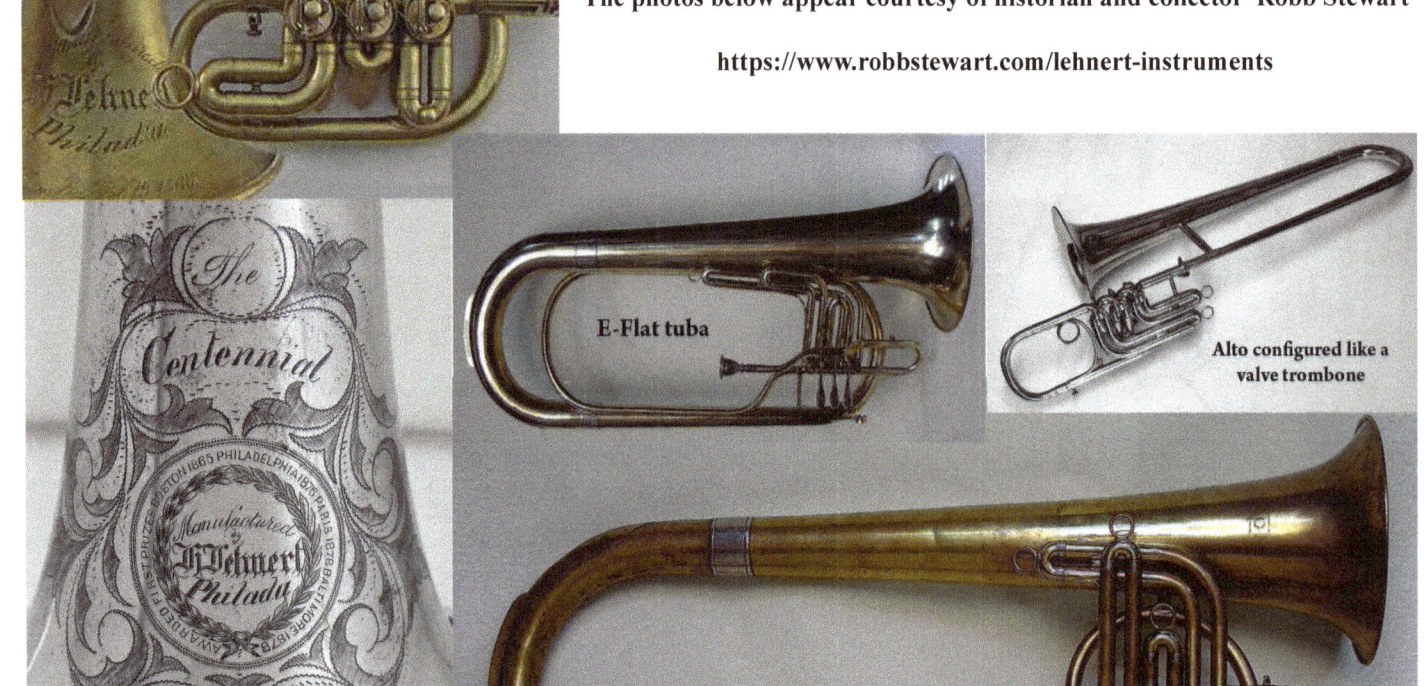

Victor J. LaPage
1906-1988

Victor LaPage (1906-1988) was born in California but spent most of his life in the Buffalo, New York, area. He invented, patented, and manufactured aluminum mutes for trumpets, trombones, and other horns before, in the 1940s, getting a patent for his design and process for brass cymbals. During WW-II LaPage worked on defense contracts and as he neared retirement age, he also repaired musical instruments for the Buffalo public schools. LaPage was a musician; a member of several orchestras and swing bands and the Buffalo Shriners band. LaPage was a Mason, an Elk, a amember of the Tuscarora club, and one of the first Commodores of the Island Yacht Club in Wilson, New York.

Although LaPage cymbals are made of brass, they are superior to the turned brass cymbals such as those produced by the Lehnert company and others. In his advertising, LaPage referred to his cymbals as Turkish-style cymbals manufactured using a closely-guarded secret process. As these cymbals do not appear to be cast, the manufacturing process is apparently a combination of turning and lathing. (Most brass cymbals do not have lathed "tone grooves" like the LaPage cymbals.) The brass alloy may be another key to the uniqueness of the LaPage cymbals. While they oxidize much like any other brass cymbals, the LaPage cymbals, when polished, are very similar in appearance to bronze cymbals.

LaPage is believed to have been active in the manufacturing of cymbals for several decades, so he probably produced many thousands of cymbals. Even now, some 60 years later, LaPage cymbals turn up regularly in the vintage instrument marketplace. Most of the LaPage cymbals have a rather distinctive flattened bell area.

The pre-WWII LaPage cymbal stamp

Post- WWII LaPage cymbal stamp

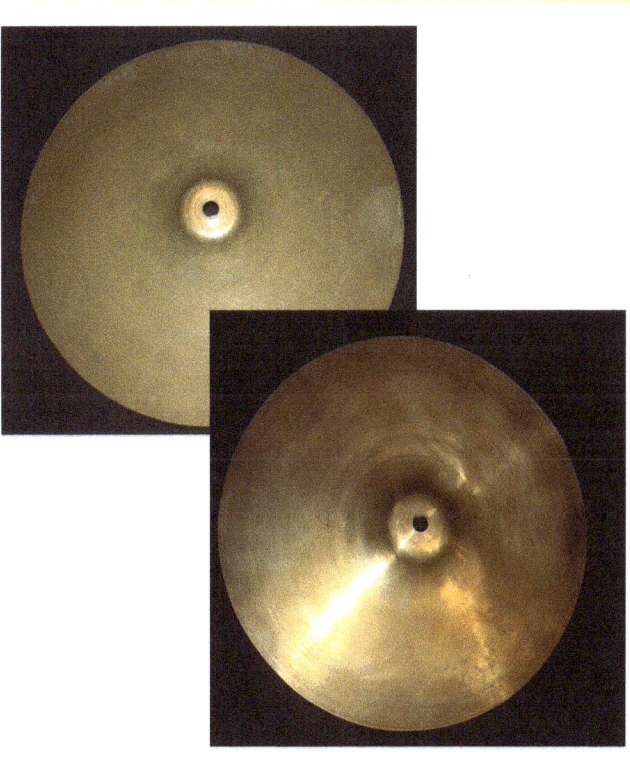

Profile of an overplayed LaPage cymbal. This is common with brass cymbals and happens when drummers try to get the cast-bronze sound from a turned brass instrument.

Profile of a LaPage cymbal with flat bell

Unpolished and polished LaPage cymbal

The first Turkish cymbal production in the United States
KAZANJIAN

Kapriel Kazanjian was born in 1861 in Antioch. (The city is known today as Antakya, Turkey.) This is in southeastern Turkey, near the Syrian border. He immigrated to the USA in 1883, listing as his occupation "manufacturer" and his industry as "Zimbils Factory".

The surname Kazanjian is a fairly common Armenian name. It is derived from the Turkish word kazanci, an occupational name for a maker or seller of (bronze) cauldrons or kettles. This indicates that the Kazanjian family had a history of working with bronze.

Kazanjian settled in the Buffalo, New York area. By 1918, Kazanjian was selling his entire production to the Wurlitzer company. Rudolph Wurlitzer owned a significant portion of the Leedy Manufacturing Company and Leedy catalogued Kazanjian cymbals from 1918 to 1924 when Kapriel was nearing retirement age.

**A Kazanjian/Wurlitzer cymbal stamp
(from a 15 inch cymbal)**

Ludwig attempts to produce Turkish cymbals

William F Ludwig (Senior) and the Wurlitzer company put a significant amount of time and money into trying to manufacture cymbals. (See page XX.) Ludwig reached out in 1919 to a metallurgy trade journal to ask for help. (Perhaps in an effort to generate a sense of urgency and some sympathy, he hinted that the very future of the cymbal-making art was at stake.)

Ludwig's 1919 letter to "The Metal Industry"

Since the war (ed note: WW-I) genuine Turkish cymbals are manufactured in or near Constantinople by Armenians.. The Armenians are the skilled workmen. They have all been driven out of Turkey or massacred. The Turks are not able to manufacture them and no one else in the world can make them. You may think this is a broad statement, but we are in the line and know of the experiments that have been carried on by ourselves and all others in our line. It will be a pity if this valuable article disappears at this time.

What we are particularly interested in is casting of cymbals such as are used in bands on bass drum. They range in diameter from 12 to 15 inches and 13 to 3/16 inch thickness making this a very difficult casting.

No one in this country is able to make cymbals by the cast process. All American cymbals are spun of sheet brass, but the quality is not nearly as good as the cast cymbals..

Previous to the ware all cast cymbals were imported from Turkey. Unless they can be manufactured in this country, we will have to resume importations of cymbals from Turkey in large quantities. We are very anxious to start manufacturing them in this country and would like your assistance if possible.

The alloy is 3 1/2 ounces tin to one pound copper, or 78% copper to 22% tin. The difficulty is in casting the cymbal in a large diameter and thin. After casting they are very hard and brittle. We know how to handle the temper proposition if you can help us out on the casting.

Kapriel Kazanjian saw Ludwig's letter and responded immediately. The next issue of "The Metal Industry" included his response.

Kazanjian response to Ludwig

To the Editor of The Metal Industry:

In the March issue of The Metal Industry on page 129 there is an article regarding "Casting Cymbals". We note that the Ludwig & Ludwig Company, drum makers, of Chicago, requested some information on how to cast cymbals, fearing that his art would be lost. I have written them that I am going to manufacture the highest grade Turkish cymbals here in America, and I have also written to all the leading houses in this respect, and I wanted to send sample cymbals, but conditions changed. After I finished my samples I submitted them to the best leading drummers and band masters. They all stated that I have the best cymbals they have ever seen in this country, and they were surprised at the high pitch and sonority of them. Now we are manufacturing them on a larger scale, and Rudolph Wurlitzer Company of Cincinnati is our sole agent, and all those interested in this famous cymbal should make inquiries regarding them direct to Wurlitzer company as our annual product is purchased by them.

THERE IS NO FEAR THAT THIS ART WILL BE LOST. All I will say is that our cymbals will be superior to the Ziljian, Constantinople make- both in appearance and in highest musical vibrations.

K. Kazanjian & Co., Buffalo, N.Y., March 24, 1919

In spite of Kazanjian's claims in his response to Ludwig, his cymbals were neither of superior quality nor available in large quantities. He explained to a newspaper reporter that he once received an order for several hundred thousand dollars worth of cymbals. The small shop that he had built was not able to produce on that scale, so he tried to fill the order by "mixing the metal" and sending it out to other shops to be cast and tempered. The cymbals they producred were brittle and broke into pieces. Kapriel explained to the reporter that at that point he had given up on the idea of being a rich man and planned to make only perfect cymbals as the proprietor of a small shop. It is not known when Kapriel Kazanjian passed away. He would have been at a retirement age when Leedy stopped listing Kazanjian cymbals in their catalogs.

THE ZILDJIAN NARRATIVE, SOURCES

Some of the authors sources are listed below. Readers are cautioned that no one source listed here is complete and 100% accurate. All, however, provide valuable insights into the complicated Zildjian narrative. Most of the books are out of print, but worth the effort to locate a copy!

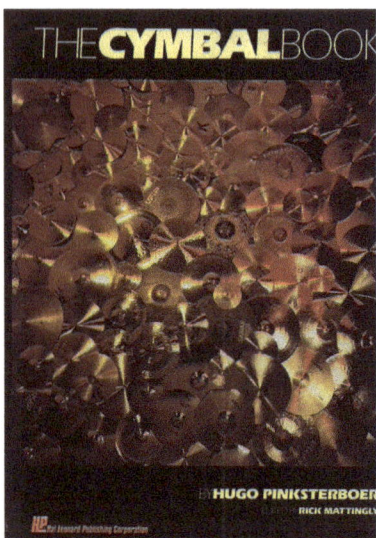

The Cymbal Book
by Hugo Pinksterboer
ISBN 0-7935-1920-9
Published in 1992, this book is a must for anyone wanting cymbal information

DRUM! Magazine
Special Collector's Edition, Feb 2012
Edited by Hugo Pinksterboer, this issue served as an update to Hugo's book which was published 20 years earlier.

Turkish Bands of Past and Present
by Pars Tuglaci
no ISBN published 1986
Parallel Turkish/English
Tuglaci is an Armenian academic, his book contains several pages on the Zildjian narrative.

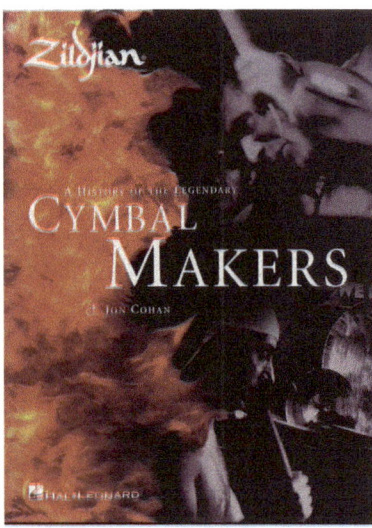

Zildjian: A History Of The Legendary Cymbal Makers
by Jon Cohan
ISBN 0-7935-9155-4, 1999

Italian Vintage Drums & Cymbals
by Luca Luciano
no ISBN, published 2012
Parallel Italian/English
Primarily drums, but excellent sections on Tosco, Ufip, and Spizzochino

Tales From The Cymbal Bag
by Lennie DiMuzio with Jim Coffin
ISBN 978-0-615-39948-5 2010
The late Lennie DiMuzio was an industry icon. His book is light on Zildjian history and manufacturing details, focus is more on anecdotes.

ARTICLES:
"Inside Sabian": Chip Stern interview with Robert Zildjian: *Modern Drummer* magazine, November, 1983

"World's Largest Cymbal Maker: Avedis Zildjian Company" by Thomas R. Navin,
Bulletin of the Business Historical Society, December 1949

THE ZILDJIAN NARRATIVE

The Zildjian family's association with the Ottoman Empire's rulers predates the very existence of the family name. The person generally recognized as the founder of the family business, Avedis Zildjian, was born on February 20, 1596. His father Kerope was reportedly the chief cauldron maker for Sultans, though we do not know exactly *which* Sultans. The cauldrons were made of bronze. These cauldrons were used to boil rice to feed the Imperial troops known as Jannisaries. There are reports of Jannisary protests which involved the troops overturning full cauldrons and beating them like drums. Many of these cauldrons are still on display in the Topkapi Palace Museum in Istanbul. Kerope also made some cymbals and his son Avedis was officially commissioned to produce cymbals for Sultan Mustafa I in 1618. At the same time, the surname of Zildjian was recognized. (Zil meaning cymbal, Zildjian roughly translates to family of cymbalsmiths.) The methods Avedis developed for casting and tempering bronze cymbals led to his establishing his own foundry and cymbal production facility in 1623.

Topkapi Palace Museum Kitchen
Some cauldrons were made of cast bronze sections riveted together (on top shelf), others were cast and hammered in one piece.

This facility was in a part of the city known as the Samatya which remains to this day a traditionally Armenian neighborhood. The key steps in the mixing and preparation of the bronze alloy was done in a "garden dungeon with iron doors" to guard the family's secret process. Mustafa I decreed the family could use the official Armenian surname of Zildjian which translates to son, or family, of cymbal smiths.

The secrets of the foundry procedures were supposedly passed on within the family, to only one male member at a time, with three family members assuming responsibility for operating the family business. Avedis had a son (Ahkam), born in 1621, who was the first relative to be entrusted with the secret process.

A GAP IN THE ZILDJIAN GENEOLOGY

All genealogical accounts of the Zildjian progression of heirs to date share a common gap between the mid 1600s, when Avedis I passed the secret process to his son Ahkamand, and the late 1800s.

We know that in 1868 a Haroutian I (Hodja Artin in Armenian) was the head of the Zildjian family and that at least 70 members of the family were employed in the family business of making cymbals.

Sultan Mustafa I
(15th Ottoman Sultan)

This information comes to us in a document in the Turkish archives found by Dr. Pars Tuglaci. The document is a petition submitted to Sultan Abdulaziz pleading for assistance for the family. They had suffered a series of fires and were considering a move to Paris to escape their debt to the Treasury. Sultan Abdulaziz agreed to the terms of a solution presented to him by his Grand Vizier; he ordered that "everything neccessary be done to help the Zildjian family."

The path of the secret formula and processes

Haroutian I passed the secret to his son Avedis II in about 1868. Avedis II did business as A. Zildjian Cie.

Avedis II, whose son Aram was too young to accept the secret, passed the secret to his brother Kerope II, who changed the business name to K Zildjian Cie.

Kerope II was in charge of the business until his passing in 1912. He ultimately passed the secret to his sons Diran and Leon.. (He had three daughters; Filor, Akabi, and Victoria.) Some versions of the Zildjian narrative claim that the secret was also shared with Aram when he became of age. This is in conflict with the narrative followed here. Sons Diran and Leon succeeded Kerope II and continued with the same name, K Zildjian Cie, until about 1914 when World War I interrupted the business. Leon died during the war, so Diran resumed by himself in 1918. Diran died in 1920 after passing the secret to his wife Hripsime. The K Zildjian production was supervised by two women (Hripsimi and Victoria) from 1920 to 1936, assisted by Akabi's son Mikael (Dulgarian) Zilcan and Filor's son Vahan (Yuzbashian) Zilcan, a silent partner.

The narrative above was the testimony of Mikael Zilcan in 1956 in New York District Court. (Gretsch/American Zildjian litigation) He testified that although he did travel to Bucharest in 1926 to help Aram establish a cymbal factory (A Zildjian Cie), he did not know the complete process until he returned to Istanbul and Victoria taught it to him in 1936. This is partially collaborated by a 1927 *Rhythm* magazine article.

The reader is reminded that throughout this whole era (from about 1913 forward), the Gretsch company was importing and distributing K Zildjian cymbals in the U.S..

**Sultan Abdul Aziz
(32nd Ottoman Sultan)**

**Sultan Abdul Hamid II
(34th Ottoman Sultan)**

The Ottomans, particularly in the early days of the empire, were quite tolerant of citizens of varied religions and ethnicities. This changed, and Armenian persecution turned to genocide under Sultan Abdul Hamid II less than a decade after the Zildjian family business had been "rescued" by Abdul Aziz. It is estimated that 100,000 to 300,000 Armenians were slaughtered between 1894 and 1896. This of course led to a certain amount of "push back" by the Armenian community, and Aram Zildjian was involved. Most Zildjian historical narratives simply mention that Aram was involved in a plot to kill the Sultan and had to flee the country. That is accurate, but the narratives usually dismiss Aram's actions as the flakey radicalism of a loner. For the record, the plot was a big deal. The group that Aram was affiliated with was the Armenian Revolutionary Federation (ARF) and the assassination attempt (known as the Yildiz assassination plot of 1905) was carefully planned and orchestrated. Around 26 people were killed, but simple dumb luck saved Abdul Hamid II when his schedule was interrupted by a conversation.

Aram fled the country for Bucharest, Rumania, where he lived for over 20 years before he established the A Zildjian & Cie cymbal company in 1926. By this time Aram was about 65 years old and, according to the sworn testimony of Mikael Zilcan in New York in 1956, he had never been engaged in the manufacture of cymbals. He formed a partnership with Mikael Zilcan and Mikael's brother-in-law Vahe Indjidjian. Aram's contribution to the partnership was the use of his name only. Indjidjian was in charge of sales, while Mikael agreed to make the cymbals. Aram gained his knowledge of cymbal production from what Mikael knew at that time.

ZILDJIAN NAME CLARIFICATIONS

For anyone researching cymbal history, it helps to recognize that different sources may use different names for the same person. Sometimes this is a translation issue. The English version of the name Haroutian sometimes appears as Hodja Artin which is the Armenian version of that same name, but spelled with English letters.

There are other reasons for name changes, most of which are seen in the various names assigned to a grandson of Kerope II who played a central role in the family business. (Kerope, you will remember, was entrusted with the secret process by his brother Avedis II whose son Aram was at the time too young. Kerope's daughter Akabi Zildjian married a man named Gabriel Dulgarian (Also sometimes spelled Dulgaryian. They named their son Mikhal.

The names of Mikhal Dulgaryian (1906-1979)
son of Akabi Zildjian (and Gabriel Dulgaryian), nephew of Victoria Zildjian

Michel Durgerian
(From a 1926 Gretsch ad) Michel is a common French translation of Michael, Durgerian is probably a simple misspelling of Dulgaryian.

Mikhail Dulgaryian
This spelling was used by Robert Zildjian when he explained the Zildjian geneology in a magazine interview. Mikhail is another translation- the English translation for this name is often Michael.

Mikhal Dulgaryian-Zildjian
Mikhal adopted the family name of his wife for obvious reasons. He was a member of the family (by marriage) and was deeply involved in the family business. It is not unusual to see both surnames when this man is referenced.

Mike Ziljian
Mike Ziljian is used by Armenian historian Pars Tuglaci in his Zildjian narrative. Mike is obviously a casual translation of the first name. It is unknown whether Ziljian is a misspelling of Zildjian. (Tuglaci misspells many names.) On a Masonic Lodge membership card belonging to Avedis III, the surname spelling is Zildjian. There is, however, a hand written memo that says, "See Ziljian". Another note on the card explains, "Sec. note. 1929: said Lawyer advises him to use this spelling as it is original way of spelling name."

Mikail Zilçan, Mikhail Zilçan, Mikail Zilcan Mikael Zilcan

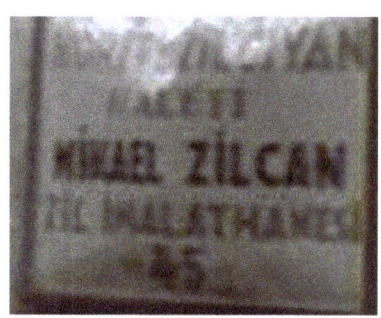

The sign above the door of Mikael Zilcan's workshop circa 1950. Translation: Cymbal workshop of Mikael Zilcan, successor to Kerope Zildjian.

Until 1934, many Turkish citizens did not have official surnames. In 1934 the Turkish government passed legislation requiring every citizen to acquire a birth certificate and declare a surname. In the fervor of new nationalism following the end of the Ottoman empire, the law forbade surnames that had non-Turkish association: "-ian" for Armenian, "-poulos" for Greek, "-off" or "-vich" for Slavs and Jews.

Mikail chose to spell his last name Zilçan. The letter ç (c with a cedilla, or tail) is used in French and Portuguese and is pronounced as an s, while c is pronounced as a k. Since the cedilla is not a thing in the English language, the name becomes Zilcan.

American Distribution

Gretsch was not the only American company to import Zildjian cymbals in the early 1900s. The Ludwig brothers listed K Zildjian & Cie cymbals in their first catalog, of 1912. (In court documents of 1956, Gretsch claims that they began importing K. Zildjian Turkish cymbals in 1913-1914.) Having started their company by manufacturing the first portable bass drum pedal, Ludwig was by 1912 making metal and wood-shelled drums, timpani, and a line of percussion accessories. William F. Ludwig invested time and money looking into the possibility of manufacturing his own cymbals. In 1919 he wrote a letter to a metallurgy trade journal asking for help. He explained that because of the turbulence in Turkish society (i.e. Armenian genocide), he was concerned that the Turkish process of cymbal making would be forever lost, and with help he could preserve this art. The aforementioned Kapriel Kazanjian responded with a letter in the next issue, stating that the art was in no danger of being lost- he was making the cymbals in Buffalo.

Ludwig was not the only American company that tried to manufacture Turkish cymbals. It was reported that the Wurlitzer company invested over $30,000.00 in the early 1900s trying to manufacture Turkish cymbals.

In 1921, Ludwig imported a massive shipment of K Zildjian & Cie cymbals. In a press release announcing the shipment, Ludwig stated that this $11,500 shipment represented the largest single batch of the cymbals ever to be imported, and that Ludwig & Ludwig were the "sole agents in America" of this brand. (In 1929, the claim was revised to a claim of being the *largest* importer of the line.)

In 1925, Fred Gretsch returned from a European business trip and gave an interview reporting on the business deals he had negotiated. He explained that he had a new manager for the Gretsch offices in Paris, and had arranged American distribution deals with a number of companies. He commented that one of the lines he expected great things from was the Zildjian brand of cymbals.

Turkish Cymbals Just Received by Ludwig & Ludwig, Chicago

The three U.S.A. Gretsch Zildjian Trademarks

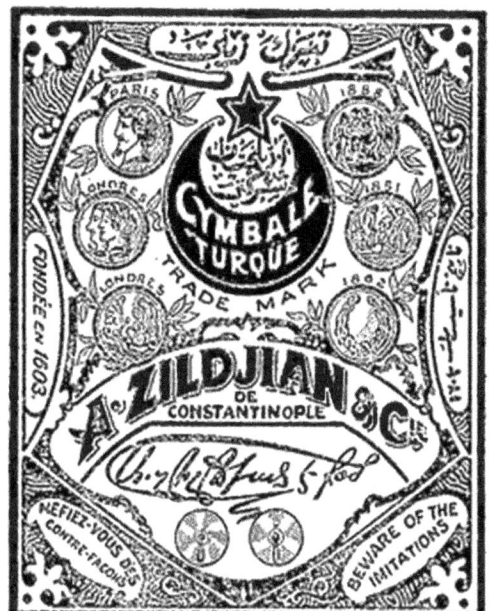

228,592
Filed September 28, 1926
Registered June 7, 1927

This trademark is for the cymbals made by Aram's Bucharest company- the company that Mikael had gone to Burcharest to help him start.. The application states that this TM had been applied to products since April 20, 1926. By the time that this trademark was registered, the company had already been dissolved. The Gretsch ownership of the trademark, however, remained in effect. This state of affairs would become a point of contention in later litigation, as it was considered abandoned after not be used for 3 years.

245,846
Filed March 13, 1928
Registered August 21, 1928

247,623
Filed March 13, 1928
Registered October 2, 1928

When Mikael Zildjian joined Aram in Bucharest, the management of the K Zildjian & Cie operation in Constantinople was assumed by the firm Ehrenstein & Toledo. (The production was supervised by Victoria.) The owner of that firm, J.S. "Yakko" Toledo, immediately arranged a trip to the USA in order to "clear up certain understandings" related to the Zildjian businesses. He explained in a November 20, 1926 interview with the American trade magazine Music Trade Review that:

1. K Zildjian & Cie is the only company in Constantinople manufacturing Turkish cymbals under the Zildjian name.
2. A firm in Bucharest has been trying without success to imitate the cymbals. Their failure was because the age-old secret of the alloy was known to only one person.
3. Despite recent claims to the contrary, K Zildjian & Cie had no exclusive selling agent in the USA. Authorized American jobbers were: C Bruno & Son, Inc., Buegeleisen & Jacobson, Carl Fischer, William R Grats Import Co., Gretsch Mfg Co., Gretsch & Brenner, Inc., Ludwig & Ludwig, and the Rudolph Wurlitzer Company.

Upon the dissolution of the Burcharest firm, Mikael returned to Constantinople where Ehrenstein & Toledo reached an agreement with Fred Gretsch, authorizing Gretsch to register these two trademarks in the USA.. This explains the filing and registration dates of the U.S.A. Gretsch Zildjian trademarks: 1926-1927 for the A. Zildjian & Cie when Aram was trying to establish his new cymbal company in Bucharest with the assistance of Mikael Zilcan, 1928 for the Zildjian and K Zildjian trademarks when Mikael had returned to Constantinople and Gretsch wanted to secure sole distribution rights.

The First Zildjian Family Split

Although Aram did not have knowledge of the secret family process for casting cymbal bronze when he left Constantinople and he did not get involved with cymbal making for nearly 20 years, his departure would come to represent the first big Zildjian family split. Victoria and her heirs would continue the K. Zildjian & Cie tradition, (REWORD THIS!) while Aram would revive the original A Zildjian & Cie name. American courts struggled with adjudicating disputes between the branches because both sides refused to reveal details of the casting process.

ARAM
son of Avedis II

VICTORIA
daughter of Kerope II

When it was time for Avedis II to pass on the secret, his son Aram was not of age, so Avedis II passed it to his younger brother Kerope II.

Aram did work in the family business, although he was not entrusted with the secret, up until 1905 when he had to flee the country. He moved to Bucharest, Rumania, where some 20 years later he started his own new company, A. Zildjian & Cie. (The same name that had been used in Constantiople in the 1800s until Kerope II changed the name to K Zildjian & Cie.when he inherited the company from Avedis II)

Aram was assisted in setting up the new A Zildjian & Cie in Bucharest by partners Mikael Zilcan and Mikael's brother-in-law Vahe Indjidjian. None of these individuals were in possession of the complete secret, but they felt they had learned enough through observing the process to start the new company.

According to court documents, Aram's contribution to the partnership was the use of his name only. Indjidjian was to act as salesman, while Mikael was to make the cymbals.

Quoting from transcripts of 1955 litigation between Gretsch and the Avedis Zildjian company: "Whatever Aram gathered concerning the formula and process was the result of watching Mikael, but since the latter did not then possess the complete secret, it follows that Aram's grasp of the subject was limited by what he was able to understand of what Mikael then knew and practiced."

Kerope II passed the secret (which he had received from his brother Avedis II) on to his sons Diran andLevon, and his daughter Victoria. Victoria had brothers and sisters involved in the family business, but in 1927 Victoria claimed to be the sole guardian of the secret process. She was assisted in operating the business at this time by Mikail Dulgaryian (Zilcan) and Vahan Yuzbashian. Yusbashian had married Filor Zildjian, another daughter of Kerope II and he later also adopted the family name Zilcan.

Gretsch had been importing and distributing K Zildjian and Cie cymbals since 1913 on a non-exclusive basis. In 1928 they arranged an agreement for exclusivity that also allowed Gretsch to register the K Zildjian & Cie trademark in the USA.

Mikail, in the course of the 1955 litigation between Gretsch and the Avedis Zildjian Company (USA), said that: "he had learned both the secret formula and process while in the employ of Victoria", but he also said that "In 1936 when Victoria revealed the secrets to him in their entirety, there were certain details which he had not previously known, and which she then imparted to him."

(ARAM, continued)

The stamp was obliterated from a K Zildjian & Cie cymbal, and it was represented as a sample of the new A Zildjian & Cie product. On the strength of this sample, A Zildjian & Cie entered into a business relationship with Fred Gretsch, who was already importing and distributing K Zildjian and Cie cymbals on a non-exclusive basis. An initial order of 100 pairs of cymbals were ordered. When the order was placed, the contract authorized Gretsch to register the A Zildjian & Cie trademark (228,592) in the USA.

When the order was received, the cymbals were found to be inferior and Gretsch made it clear there would be no further orders. (The trademark was never really used. When it was not renewed, it was judged as abandoned, and and was many years later acquired by the American Avedis Zildjian Company.)

Aram continued to make cymbals in Burcharest, under the A Zildjian name, while Gretsch made it clear in their advertising that the only genuine Zildjian cymbals were the K Zildjian cymbals. It is not known for sure whether Aram ever returned to Constantinople (or Istanbul; the city's name change was in 1930.) The famous letter that he wrote to Avedis III, who was in the USA, suggesting an American partnership venture, was written from Bucharest in 1927. The partnership was formed in the USA listing three partners; Aram, Armand (Avedis III), and Puzant, the brother of Armand (Avedis III).

AVEDIS ARMAND ZILDJIAN (1888-1979)
Avedis III, father of Robert and Armand

This is the "Avedis" credited with starting the American cymbal business, so for the sake of brevity, he will be referred to simply as Avedis.

Avedis was not involved in the family business in his homeland of Turkey. He was born in 1888 and was the nephew of Aram. He had an opportunity to accompany a wealthy Armenian family's son to America and immigrated in 1908. His brother Puzante (8 years younger) immigrated in 1922. Avedis had established a candy business and was operating that when Aram approached him about starting a new cymbal company in the USA. An awkward aspect of this situation was that Gretsch owned the trademark rights to both A Zildjian & Cie and K Zildjian & Cie. as well as the name "Zildjian". There was litigation over the matter. The judgement was made that Avedis could use the Zildjian name on his cymbals, but only if they included the trademark "Avedis Zildjian & Co. Cymbals Made in U.S.A."

Changes of ownership of the Turkish Zildjian company and Zildjian Trademarks

As explained on page XX in the section explaining the three Gretsch Zildjian trademarks, ownership of the Turkish factory and it's trademarks had been assumed by Ehrenstein & Toledo in the 1920s. Also in the 1920s, they granted permission to Gretsch (as a Zildjian distributor) to register Zildjian trademarks *for the USA*.

In the 1940s, the Turkish company got into financial trouble and was bailed out by Yakko Toledo's son-in-law, Sali Kovo. Kovo at that time became the owner and general manager.

There would be many legal battles (see pp xx) over trademark rights; primarily between Gretsch (as the owner of USA Trademark rights to K Zildjian & Cie, A Zildjian & Cie, and the word ZILDJIAN) and the Avedis Zildjian company. Robert Zildjian would later comment that he tried to convince his father that the biggest competitive threat to the Avedis Zildjian cymbal company was the Paiste company, but Avedis remained obsessed with obtaining the K Zildjian marque.

In 1963 Avedis III tried to negotiate with Kovo in an attempt to acquire the Turkish company. There was a huge argument, and the negotiations stopped.

Fred Gretsch Jr. sold the Gretsch Mfg Co. to Baldwin in 1967.* This meant that Baldwin became the owner of the two Zildjian trademarks (245846 & 247643) and continued to distribute K. Zildjian cymbals that were actually being manufactured by the Avedis Zildjian Company which had been fighting for years to acquire these trademarks.

In 1968 the negotiations between the Avedis Zildjian Company and Kovo were reopened. This time it was Robert Zildjian who negotiated on behalf of the Avedis Zildjian Company, assisted by Tony Wallace who worked for Percussion S.A., the Avedis Zildjian Company's European distribution firm. They were successful in acquiring, on behalf of the Avedis Zildjian Company, the K. Zildjian Company and all of the European trademarks. They also made yet another attempt in the American Courts to get the trademarks xxxxxx and xxxxx away from (Baldwin) Gretsch.

The 1968 litigation left trademarks xxxxx and xxxxx with (Baldwin) Gretsch, (See page xx) The ownership of these trademarks would finally shift to Zildjian in 1973 when Robert Zildjian (check- Armand?) arranged with Baldwin a 10-year exclusive distribution agreement for K. Zildjian cymbals in exchange for Baldwin giving up its trademark rights to the Avedis Zildjian company.

Through all of this, the Turkish factory continued supplying K. Zildjian cymbals to Gretsch in the USA. This continued until 1975 when, in the words of Robert Zildjian, "things became impossible with the Turkish government." Robert went to (Baldwin) Gretsch and explained that the production of K Zildjian cymbals would be moving to the Canadian plant of the Avedis Zildjian company.

Charlie Roy attempted to buy the Kustom/Gretsch company from Baldwin in 1982 and managed the division for a little over two years. This was not a successful enterprise, and a bankruptcy ensued. Fred W. Gretsch (nephew of Fred Gretsch Jr.) became the new owner of the Gretsch Company, taking possession on Jan 1, 1985. The Gretsch Company was now again owned by the family of it's founder, but no longer owned the Zildjian trademarks. (They *did,* however, retain ownership of the Ajaha trademark, but that is another story...)

* The sale to Baldwin and sequence of events during the Baldwin era are detailed in *The Gretsch Drum Book*.

CYMBAL WARS

Events outlined in the previous few pages were accompanied by a great deal of litigation- mainly in the United States courts. The primary litigants were the "new" U.S. Zildjian company, and the Gretsch company which had become the exclusive U.S. distribtutor (and trademark owner) of the Turkish Zildjian company.

The author is not a lawyer, and the litigation outlined here is not a comprehensive directory of *all* litigation. The author bears no malevolence toward any of the individuals or companies involved in these disputes. The goal is to correct some misleading (but widely repeated and accepted) narratives that have been created over the last century. The actions outlined here are meant to give the reader a basic understanding of the evolution of the cymbal industry in the United States.

1929 Decree

from the action entitled: The Fred Gretsch Mfg. Co., Plaintiff v. Aram Zildjian, Armand Zildjian and P. Zildjian, co-partners, doing business under the name of A. Zildjian & Co., Defendants.

The first paragraph of this decree reads:

"Ordered, Adjudged, and Decreed that Plaintiff (Gretsch) is the sole and exclusive owner of the certificate of registration of trade marks issued to plaintiff on the 17th day of June, 1927, No. 228,592; on the 21st day of August, 1928, No. 245,846, and on the 2nd day of October, 1928, No. 247,623 and of the trade marks therein and thereby registered and each of them and of all the rights secured by the aforesaid certificates of registration."

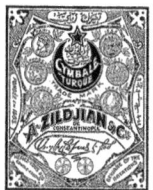

228,592

247,623

"ZILDJIAN"

245,846

As explained in the preceding pages, the Gretsch company secured trademarks on A Zildjian Co. in 1927, K Zildjian Co. in 1928, and the word Zildjian in 1928. When Aram Zildjian came to the U.S. in 1928 for the express purpose of establishing a new cymbal company with his nephews Armand (Avedis) and his brother Puzante, Gretsch filed a complaint with the District Court of the U.S. for the district of Massachusetts. The result was this consent decree dated September 19, 1929, that acknowledged the validity of all three of the Gretsch trademarks. The decree did authorize the new American partnership limited use of their Zildjian family name; *"provided it was always preceded by the full first name of any Zildjian associated with the company and the words "Made in U.S.A." were prominently stamped on the cymbals."* The new company was expressly forbidden to use the name "A. Zildjian & Co." or "K. Zildjian & Co."

The decree went on to spell out that its terms would remain in effect for as long as the currently existing trademark registrations remained in effect. It was noted that should any of the trademarks fall into disuse, *then* the Plaintiffs may make use of them.

1953
Avedis Zildjian Company v. The Fred Gretsch Mfg Co.

Note: Beginning with this litigation, this Plaintiff is referred to as a corporate entity, successor to the partnership identified in the 1929 decree.

Gretsch had registered the A Zildjian & Cie trademark (228,592) in 1926-1927 when they intended to import and distribute the cymbals Aram Zildjian was making in Burcharest. It is not clear whether the letter "A" represented "Aram" or whether it was a resurrected version of the "A Zildjian Cie" name used by Avedis II in the late 1860s. When Gretsch backed away from this relationship in favor of registering the "K" and "Zildjian" trademarks in 1928, they abandoned usage of the A Zildjian & Cie trademark. After three years of disuse, the trademark was legally considered abandoned. When the Avedis Zildjian Company tried to register the abandoned trademark in their own name, they also tried to gain ownership of the other two trademarks "K" (247,623) and "Zildjian" (245,826).

The commissioner of Patents issued a ruling on April 2, 1953 rejecting all of these claims. The Avedis Zildjian company immediately filed a complaint with the U.S. District Court, in July of 1953.

1956
Avedis Zildjian Company v. The Fred Gretsch Mfg Co.
United State District Court E.D. New York Civ. No. 13728

In this action, the Avedis Zildjian Company asks the U.S. Patent Office to cancel (and deny renewal registration of) two of the three Gretsch Zildjian trademarks- the third having been abandoned by Gretsch. The principal argument given was that the trademarks should never have been granted in the first place, as Gretsch was not the manufacturer of the cymbals, but merely the agent of the Turkish producer. This argument was supported by referrals to later Patent Office holdings having to do with importers of trade mark articles. Decisions were cited to the effect that an importer of goods bearing a trade mark of a foreign manufacturer is NOT the owner of the trade mark and therefore not eligible to register it with the United States Patent Office. In other words, the argument was that the 1953 Decree had become obsolete in light of later departmental holdings.

The ruling of the court regarding this argument was that Gretsch had been much more than a mere importer and their 1928 contract with the Turkish factory K Zildjian & Co. called for Gretsch to develop and expand business in the United States and Canada of the Turkish producer. The good will of the business was assigned to Gretsch for the purpose of effectuating its right to register the trademarks in question.

A second argument presented by the Zildjian Company was that the secret formula and process practiced by Kerope Zildjian had become the property of this plaintiff. In other words, the Zildjian company was claiming that Aram Zildjian was the rightful heir and owner of the secret formula and process.

To this second argument, Gretsch responded with testimony from Mikael Zildjian detailing the line of succession of the secret process and formula. (See page **XX The path of the secret formula and processes**)

The ruling of the court was that the provisions of the consent decree remained in full force and effect. The ruling also verified that the A Zildjian & Cie (A Zildjian & Co.) trademark 228,592 had been cancelled by action of the United States Patent Office and that by virtue of the provisions of the 1929 decree, the Avedis Zildjian Co. had the legal right to use the trademark. (If their registration application was approved, which would not happen.)

The above explanation is an abbreviated narrative of the litigation. There was also an allegation of fraud on the part of Gretsch, and a number of counterclaims by Gretsch against the Avedis Zildjian Company. The allegation and counterclaims were all dismissed.

1958
Avedis Zildjian Co., Plaintiff-appellant v the Fred Gretsch Mfg Co., Defendant-appellee
251 F. 2d530 (2d Cir. 1958)

This action is an appeal by both parties of the rulings in the litigation of 1956.

The court's ruling included a summary of the situation that led to this action:

During the 1920s, two branches of the Zildjian family were producing cymbals. One branch was located in Turkey, the other in Rumania. Both sold cymbals to and through the defendant (Gretsch) and authorized the defendant (Gretsch) to register in the United States various trademarks incorporating the word "Zildjian". The defendant obtained a number of registrations pursuant to these arrangements. The cymbals of the Rumanian Zildjians proved somewhat less than perfect, however, and after the Rumanian firm of A Zildjian & Cie was dissolved in 1926, Aram Zildjian, one of it's partners, came to the United States, where he formed a partnership with his nephew Avedis Zildjian, to manufacture cymbals. That company was the plaintiff's predecessor.

Troubles ensued with two Zildjians manufacturing cymbals for distribution in the United States. Both used the name "Zildjian" to identify their products, which each claimed (and still claim) were the only cymbals made according to the ancient family process. Litigation resulted in a consent decree entered in 1929. That decree has not brought peace.

This appeal is a continuation of the Avedis Zildjian Company's efforts to cancel Gretsch's ownership of Zildjian trademarks. The four grounds cited are very similar to the grounds used by the Avedis Zildjian Company in prior litigation:
1. The Defendant (Gretsch) never owned the trademarks in the first place and therefore could not register them.
2. The Defendant (Gretsch) has abandoned the trademarks.
3. The Defendant (Gretsch) fraudulently obtained renewal of the marks by falsely swearing that they were still in use.
4. The trademark "Zildjian" had become a grade mark.

This appeal also includes 2 counterclaims against the Avedis Zildjian Company by the defendant Gretsch:
1. Avedis Zildjian Company has conducted acts of unfair competition and violations of the 1929 decree.
2. Avedis Zildjian Company has fraudulently registered certain trademarks in Canada.

The court dismissed all four of these claims, and both of the counterclaims.

1968

394 F.2d 860; 157 USPQ 517

This is an appeal by the Avedis Zildjian Company of the refusal of the Trademark and Appeal board to allow the registration by the Avedis Zildjian company of the abandoned A Zildjian & Cie trademark referenced in the 1929 decree and subsequent litigation.

Ed. Note: The Gretsch family sold Gretsch Mfg. Co. to the Baldwin company in 1967.

Baldwin continued to operate the company as a division of Baldwin, and continued to defend the Zildjian trademarks granted to Gretsch in the 1920s.

The A. Zildjian & Cie trademark #228592 was originally registed by Gretsch for the cymbals produced by Aram Zildjian's Romanian form and to be exclusively distributed in the USA by Gretsch. The initial batch of cymbals was found to be unacceptable, and Gretsch ordered no more cymbals. The trademark fell into disuse, and was therefore considered abandoned after three years. The Avedis Zildjian Company of the USA sought to register the trademark in their own name in 1959 but the Trademark Trial and Appeal board rejected the application on the grounds that this would cause confusion with the two other Zildjian trademarks registered in the name of the Fred Gretsch Manufacturing Company.

This appeal sought to reverse that rejection. Among the arguments presented was a reminder that the 1929 Decree specifically allowed for the Avedis Zildjian Company's use of any of the three trademarks should they be cancelled.

In it's decision, the court stated: *"We think that the following is an accurate summary of this court's views as expressed in former opinions.* ***The interests of the public may not be ignored; and when it appears that the goods are so nearly related that their sale under identical trade marks would be likely to confuse the public or to deceive purchasers, registration must be denied notwithstanding the owner's consent."***

The judges presiding over this appellant litigation were a chief judge and four other judges. One of the judges, a Judge Smith, explained in his opinion that he had a separate and distinct reason for refusing the "right" of the Avedis Zildjian Company to register the trademark on the basis of the 1929 Decree.

From his statement:

Before a right to use [a trademark] can be predicated on a court decree, it is necessary to show identity of the parties or to establish privity such that the party asserting the right is clearly entitled to exercise the rights granted therein. Appellants case fails at this point. I am unwilling to assume that the present record establishes identity of appellant and the defendants named in the decree of September 19, 1929 or any showing of privity between them.

The consent decree to which the majority opinion and Judge Rich's dissent refer was entered in an action in which the parties defendant were three individuals, "Aram Zildjian, Armand Zildjian, and P. Zildjian" designated in the application as "Avedis Zildjian & Co., a corporation duly organized under the laws of the Commonwealth of Massachusetts." The declaration accompanying the application is signed by one "Avedis Zildjian" as president of that corporation.

Who was P. Zildjian?

The initial litigation between the American Zildjian company and Gretsch listed as plaintiffs "Aram Zildjian, Armand Zildjian, and P. Zildjian" designated as "Avedis Zildjian & Co". "Armand" Zildjian was Armand Avedis Zildjian, who would soon become known simply as Avedis, or Avedis III. "P. Zildjian" was Puzante Zildjian, older brother of Avedis III. Puzante was born on July 4, 1896 in Turkey. Avedis III was born three years later in 1889, also in Turkey. Avedis III immigrated to the USA in 1910, Puzante immigrated twelve years later in 1922, evidently to join Avedis III in his successful candy company. His "Declaration of Intention" filed with the Naturalization Service upon entering the USA listed his occupation as "Candy Maker". He swore that he intended to become a citizen of the USA and permenantly reside in the USA.

When Aram came to the USA to form the cymbal company with Avedis III and Puzante, he came on a temporary visa, stating that he planned to be in the US for 6 months. Aside from being a principal partner in the family cymbal business along with Aram and Avedis III, Puzante did not play an active role in the operating of the company or the manufacturing of cymbals. When Avedis III died in 1979, Puzante had predeceased him in 1965.

Zildjian finally acquires the American Zildjian Trademarks

The Baldwin Company, under Lucyn Wolzin, was not nearly as invested in defending the American Zildjian trademarks 245846 and 247623 as the Gretsch family had been. They were a conglomerate with bigger fish to fry. It has been reported that another factor in settling this dispute was that Armand Zildjian had a very good social relationahip with Wolzin. By 1973, Baldwin signed the rights to the trademarks over to Zildjian. The price? The Zildjian company agreed to give (Baldwin) Gretsch exclusive distribution rights for a period of 10 years. Since (Baldwin) Gretsch already had an ongoing exclusive distribution deal, this deal mean that (Baldwin) Gretsch essentially agreed to give the rights to Zildjian for free, in 10 years.

Another Zildjian Family Split

Avedis Zildjian had struggled to consolidate the business interests of the Zildjian family for virtually his entire adult life. He gained ownership of the Turkish K Zildjian Factory in 1968. He finally acquired all of the Zildjian trademarks by 1973. He shifted production of the K Zildjian cymbals from Turkey to Canada in 1975.

When Avedis died in 1979, he passed ownership of the company to his two sons Robert and Armand. They each received 49.472 percent ownership with the remainder going into a trust controlled by both men.

Robert and Armand were both very strong-willed individuals with very different personalities. Robert once explained that when he and his brother were operating the company along with their father, it was easier to settle difference; whichever brother Avedis sided with won the day. With the passing of Avedis in1979, settling differences became more difficult.

Robert and Armand parted ways. After two years of separation litigation, the settlement called for Armand to continue with the Avedis Zildjian factory in Boston, while Robert used the Canadian factory to start his new cymbal company SABIAN, an acronym for his three children Sally, Billy, and Andy. Terms of the settlement called for Sabian to not enter the world cymbal market until January of 1982, and to not enter the USA cymbal market until January of 1983.

The Avedis Zildjian Company updates- TBA

Sabian updates- TBA

Post-Zildjian Turkish Cymbal Production

The American branch of the Zildjian family finally acquired all the the Zildjian trademarks and Turkish facilities in 1968. Mikael continued making cymbals in the Istanbul factory, and these K Zildjian cymbals continued to be shipped from Istanbul to Gretsch as the exclusive American distributor. In 1975, the American Zildjian family closed the Turkish factory. They notified Gretsch of the decision, and informed them that key workers from the Istanbul factory would be brought to the Canadian cymbal manufacturing facility (AZCO) and the K Zildjian cymbals would be manufactured there. By 1977, the Turkish Zildjian factory was closed and the manufacturing equipment was scrapped.

Mikael passed away a couple of years later, in 1979. (A few months after the passing of Avedis Zildjian III in the USA.) At the time of his retirement and the dissolution of the Turkish Zildjian factory, Mikael was not in sole possession of the "secret process". Some of his employees had been working with him for decades and were considered master cymbal smiths. Probably the first of those workers to "reopen the factory" (to use their words) were Mehmet Tamdeger and Agop Tomurcuk. They had begun working for Mikael when they were young boys of about 8 years old in 1949, so they had almost 30 years of training in all phases of cymbal manufacturing. The "secret process" was no longer a closely guarded family secret, but a process that was known and shared by numerous former Zildjian employees, and the employees of the new companies that they created. The diagram below illustrates *some* of the ways in which the Turkish cymbal industry continued to fracture. It does not attempt to document the many OEM brand names that these companies produced.

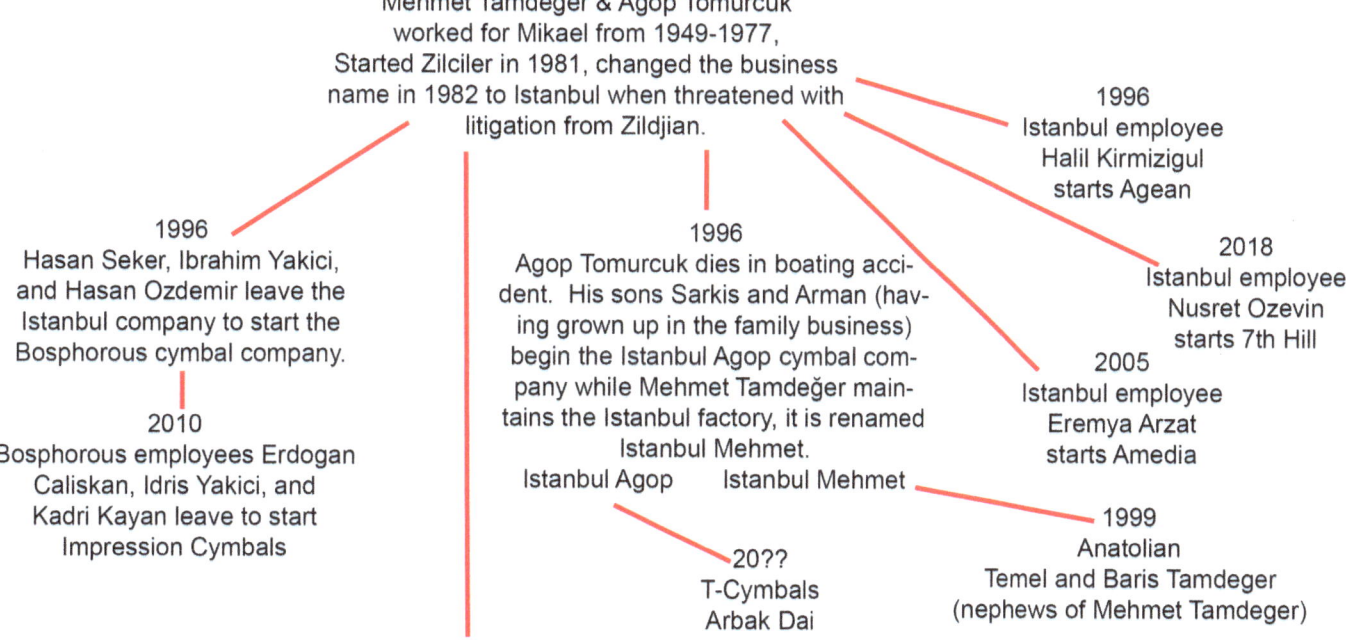

Brothers Ibrahim and Murat Diril and their cousin Mustafa moved from Samsun to Istanbul in the late 1980s with other family members. They were all trained by Mehmet and Agop in the early 1990s, working under them for about five years. By 1999 they had all moved back to Samsun to make cymbals together and they collaborated with Meinl on the Byzance series and with Paiste on the Twenty series. A fourth brother, Adem, also worked at Meinl from 2006 to 2021 All four eventually started their own cymbal companies:

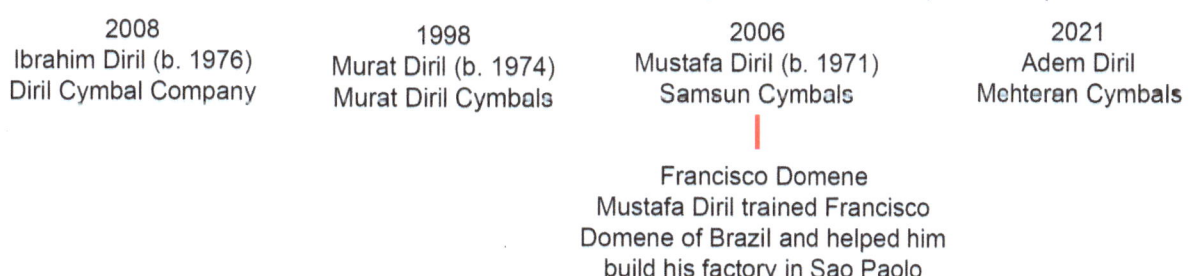

The Independant Craftsman Movement

In the late 1990s and early 2000s, the number of independant cymbal craftsmen began to dramatically increase. Many were inspired by artists such as Roberto Spizzichino whose mastery of the hammering and lathing skills were creating great sounding cymbals. The "movement" was helped along by the increased competition in the cymbal market. Cymbal companies with foundries became willing to sell "blanks", or unfinished cymbals, and found a growing market. Another boost came from the members of this group themselves as they encouraged each other. This information exchange began to reach a wider public with the creation of an online bulletin-board called Cymbalholic by Chad Anderson. The forum was active from July of 2001 to May of 2019. The "biggest" years were around 2004-2005 There was a major computer crash that lost a lot of data but much was recovered. From 2010 to 2019, it was largely kept afloat by users. .

Cymbalholic

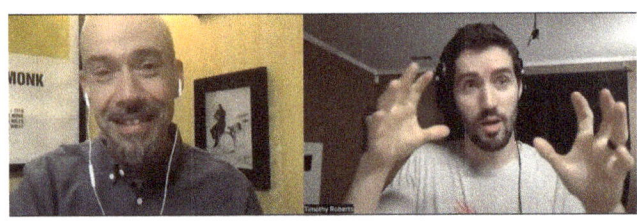

Cymbalholic founder Chad Anderson interviewed by Timothy Roberts. The QR code and link lead to the youtube interview.

Cymbalholic founder Chad Anderson interviewed by Dave Collingwood. The QR code and link lead to the youtube interview.

Link:
https://www.youtube.com/watch?v=9xlAJVdty9g

Link:
https://www.youtube.com/watch?v=uQf-zUORLMM

This QR code is a link to the touching and eloquent memorial message that the late Mike Skiba's daughter Kayla posted when he passed.

Michael Skiba
2-13-1960 / 11-13-2010

Clearly Mike worked as hard at his communication skills as he did at his craft of cymbalsmithing. He informed and educated through his posts at the Cymbalholic forum. Although the forum does not exist at this writing, there is am active Facebook page for fans of Mike Skiba:
https://www.facebook.com/groups/1739544219693027
Also compilations of his Cymbalholic posts have been posted online in PDF form.

Excerpts from Mike Skiba's Cymbalholic Forum posts:

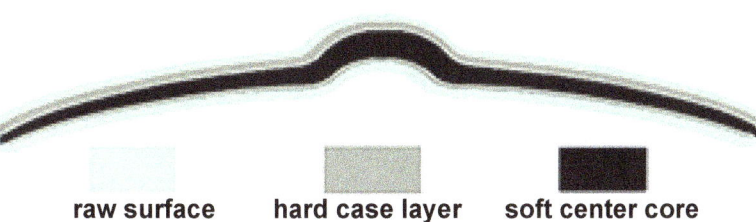

LAYERS OF A CYMBAL BLANK

The rolling and annealing processes create a condition of stratified metal that is harder (more dense) at the surfaces, where the metal had the greatest reaction to the differences in temperature. Trapped inside the top and bottom surfaces is softer metal that was insulated from the intense heat, and thus slower to react...this metal is less musical, but more consistent and pliable. We now have a total of 5 layers of gradient hardness, from the two extreme (oxidized) raw surfaces to the hard case layers beneath each of these, to the softer center core layer. These layers "want" to naturally equalize with each other...after all, they are made of the same material, but their physical properties typically differ to such an extent that they will ultimately retain much/most of their unique qualities. It's also interesting to note that blanks made at different weights/ thicknesses will exhibit different layering. Very thin pieces will tend to cook almost all the way through, while very heavy blanks come through with a greater percentage of softer core material. This also means that they have different respective futures... during and after manufacture.

THE FUNDAMENTAL KEY TO A GOOD CYMBAL IN TENSION

*Tension exists in numerous forms and can be created by numerous processes...each has different effects over time. A blank piece of metal becomes a cymbal when it is forced to store tension...this is where the metal begins to ring in a musical manner. The very first incidence of applied-by-design tension is pressing of the bell, which sets up a point of anchorage against which future installation of designed tension can pull. While it may be argued that the first application of heat during rolling causes tension, I find this too vague as it escapes the criteria of proper design...it is merely a rudimentary process that has side-effects. The act of pressing the bell is done with control, expecting a specific outcome and literally creating a "cymbal within a cymbal". The bell is also a critical area that often finds itself dealing with the effects of time separately from the main body of a cymbal... we've all seen plenty of bridge cracks and spiders at the bell-hole. In many of these cases the entire body of the cymbal remains completely intact, unaffected by the disasters happening "upstairs". Many cracks at the bridge are the result of tension that overcomes the anchor, where the anchor lets go. In my mind, spider cracks at the center hole are analogous to blowing a tweeter, where the amplifier (bell) has "clipped" past it's capacity to transmit sudden transient vibration. Keep in mind the tension located in the bell is greater than anywhere else in a cymbal, so it stands to reason that the metallic bonds have the odds already stacked against them.
When all the manufacturing processes have been completed we have a finished cymbal, but the metal is not finished...not by a long shot. In most production environments the cymbal FINALLY gets a chance to sit down and relax, often housed in "vaults" that may even be climate-controlled so as to establish a stable atmosphere for rest and relaxation. In theory all of the manufacturing operations before were carried out to include the anticipation of rest, free of vibration. The commonly accepted term "aged-in" may begin now, as the clock continues to tick. This is a tricky term for me, as I see a distinct difference between "aged-in" as opposed to "played-in", as well as a combination of the two.*

Cymbal Companies and Smiths

This list excludes many companies and cymbal smiths of the past who are no longer in business.

Such a list becomes out of date almost as soon as it is compiled. If anyone is aware of updates, changes, or additions that should be made to this list, please contact Rob Cook; rob@rebeats.com.

This list includes:
Individual Smiths who create cymbals by hammering and lathing finished cymbals and/or blanks.
Companies who design cymbals which they have manufactured for them.
Artists who create "sound sculptures"

37 Cymbals	USA
7th Hill	Turkey
Espen Aalberg	Norway
AG Custom Cymbals	USA
Agazarian	China
Agean Cymbals	Turkey
Ajaha	USA
Alla Turca Cymbals	Turkey
Amedia Cymbals	Turkey
Anatolian Cymbals	Turkey
Arborea	China
ArtCymbal Manabu Yamamoto	Japan
Artisan-Turk	Turkey
Asabag, Netanel	Israel
Berpson	China
BFC Brazilian Finest Cymbals	Brazil
Matt Bettis	USA
Big Island Cymbals	Hawaii
Borba Cymbals	USA
Bosphorus Cymbals	Turkey
Mattia Bourgis	Spain
Brasswood	Netherlands
Marius Buck	Germany
Buffalo Cymbals	USA
Burke's Works	USA
Byrne Cymbals Ray Byrne	USA
Ariel Calabria	USA
Lance Campeau	Canada
Cech, Alexino	Austria
Centent	China
Champion Cymbals	New Zealand
Collingwood Cymbals	UK
Constantine Cymbals	Turkey
Cymatic Cymbals	USA
Cymbal and Gong	Turkey
Cymbal Craftsman (Paul Francis)	USA
Cymbalatelier	Singapore
Cymbalutopia Craig Lauritson	Australia
Defiant Cymbal Company	Mexico
Helge Dichanz	Netherlands
Diril Cymbals Ibrahim Diril	Turkey
Murat Diril	Turkey
Dream Cymbals & Gongs	China
Emjmod	Japan
Mike Ernst Cymbals	USA
Funch Cymbals	Denmark
Frank Gegerle	Germany
Gio Cymbals	Turkey
Alessandro Gioiello	Italy
GM Designs Cymbals	USA
Domen Godec Cymbals	Slovenia
Hayden Cymbals	USA
Head Custom Cymbals	Italy
Heartbeat Percussion	Turkey
Hershko Cymbals	Israel
Homemade Cymbals	Germany
Steve Hubback	Netherlands
Imperial Cymbals	Turkey
Impression Cymbals	Turkey
Istanbul Agop	Turkey
Istanbul Mehmet	Turkey
Istanbul Pera	Turkey
Johan Nicolas Janicke	France
KL Custom Cymbals	Croatia
Kamin Cymbals	Germany
Kasza Cymbals	Turkey
Gregg Keplinger	USA
Olver Kern Cymbals	Germany
Kmicic Cymbals	Poland
Koide	Japan
Kupo Cymbals	Singapore
David La Mela	Belgium
Legado Cymbals	Turkey
Stefan Leibinger	Germany

Leon Cymbals	Turkey
Kruno Levacic	Croatia
Lius Cymbals	Sweden
F. Madejski Cymbals Mfr	Poland
Marcus Cymbals	Argentina
Masterwork	Turkey
Mehteran	Turkey
Meinl	Germany
Mike Mongiello	USA
Morlang Percussion	Germany
Morris Cymbal Arts	USA
Muysk Cymbals	Colombia
Moon Baby Walking Gongs	USA
Silvio Morger	Germany
Nebulae Cymbals	Indonesia
Matt Nolan	UK
Nugis	Russia
Omete Cymbals	China
Orion Cymbals	Brazil
Ottaviano	USA
S.P. Parkkinen Cymbals	Finland
Pergamon	Turkey
PGB	Canada
Paiste	Switzerland
Michael Paiste	Switzerland
Pantheon Percussion	Turkey
PUG Cymbals	Australia
Quijano Cymbals	Belgium
Quiqeg	Italy
Timothy Roberts (Reverie Drum Co)	USA
Royal Cymbals	(see Cymbal Craftsman)
Ryet Cymbals	India
Sabian	Canada
Sagurton, J David	USA
Saluda Cymbals	USA
Samsun	Turkey
Bruno Schell	Brazil
Scymtek	Turkey
Seifried Cymbals (steve)	USA
Shelledy Sounds	USA
SIHI	Finland
Silken	China
Jesse Simpson	Czech Republic
Skretas Family Cymbal Company	USA
Smyrna Cymbals	Turkey
Soultone Cymbals	Turkey
Spectrum Cymbals	USA
Stagg Cymbals	China
Supernatural Cymbals	Turkey
TongXiang Cymbals	China
Tonum	Russia
T-Cymbals	Turkey
TRX Cymbals	Turkey
Trakian Cymbals	Turkey
Trexist Cymbals	Turkey
Trinity Cymbals	China
Tunyo Cymbals	Poland
Turco	Turkey
Turkish Cymbals	Turkey
Ufip	Italy
V Classic	Turkey
Vansir Cymbals	China
Julian Vleminkx	Belgium
Wuhan	China
Xilxo Erce Gokhan	Turkey
Zarras Cymbals	USA
Zildjian	USA
Zilli Cymbals	Turkey
Zultan	Turkey

Cymbal stores:

Memphis Drum Shop

The Cymbal House (Cincy)

Sounds Anatolian
https://soundsanatolian.com

The Cymbal Boutique

Cymbal Swap Shop

Round Sounds

Maxwell Drums

37 CYMBALS
USA
https://www.facebook.com/37Cymbals
Heather Stine littlemisspunkass@gmail.com

7th Hill
Turkey
https://www.7th-hill.com/

We believe in music. We believe in sound. And we strongly believe in the rich heritage of Turkish cymbal making.

7th Hill aims to create meaningful additions to that ancient history. Starting out with a limited number of series that will satisfy your appetite for great sounding cymbals in any style of music, we have great ideas for years to come.

Just stay around.
Just listen.
And keep on playing in the meantime.

Nusret Özevin started 7th Hill in the spring of 2018. He was closely involved with Istanbul Cymbals from the very beginning in 1984, and he has been in and around the fascinating world of cymbals ever since.

The name of this new company is a humble tribute to the Istanbul quarter that housed the world's most famous cymbal factory for many years: Samatya, the seventh hill.

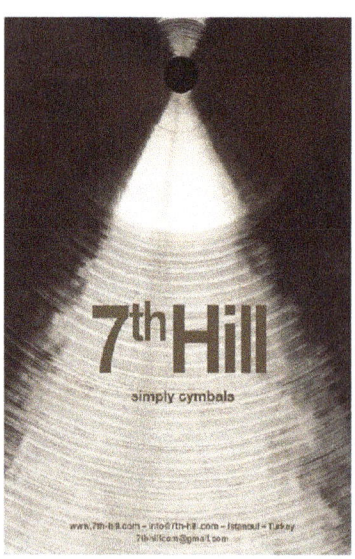

AG CUSTOM CYMBALS
USA
Andrew Green, Chicago
@agcustomcymbals

ESPEN AALBERG
Norway
https://www.instagram.com/eaalberg/
https://www.facebook.com/espen.aalberg

Espen Aalberg, 47, is a Norwegian jazz musician known for his contributions in several orchestras like The Core, Shagma, Kwaz, Håvard Lund Quartet and musicians like Jonas Kullhammar, Håvard Wiik, and Torbjörn Zetterberg.
He also contributes on a series of recordings.
Albums: Basement Sessions Vol.1, Basement Sessions, Vol. 3 (The Ljubljana Tapes), Sommer i Lufta
Music groups: The Core, Norwegian Air Force Band

AGAZARIAN
China
Agazarian cymbals and gongs are from the Hubei Province of China from B20 bronze and individually crafted by hand in a centuries-old tradition. Agazarian cymbals are considered by many to be an entry-level cymbals, are inexpensive compared to average hand-hammered B20 cymbals, and are often stocked by the "Big Box" retailers.

AGEAN CYMBALS
Turkey
https://ageancymbals.com/

Istanbul employee Halil Kirmizigul started Agean in 1996

AJAHA
Italy

Trademark 800,367 Ajaha

Serial number 193,357 filed May 13, 1964, registered December 14, 1965

    The first U.S. Trademark granted to Gretsch for cymbals appears to be for Ajaha cymbals. The 1965 Trademark registration indicates that the first use was in 1922. The 1912 Gretsch catalog indicates that Ajaha was already a U.S. Government registered trademark at that time, but the Trademark office does not have accessible records for that era. Ajaha cymbals were presented as Turkish cymbals, later catalogs described them as "turkish style cymbals." They apparently were always manufactured in Italy. In a 1925 Music Trades article, Fred Gretsch Sr. is quoted as referring to them as Tuscany (a region in Italy) cymbals. By the 1950s Gretsch's Ajaha cymbals were being made in Italy by Ufip and in the 1970s by the Italian firm Tosco.

    Although Ajaha cymbals are not being manufactured or distributed at this writing the Trademark is still active and owned by Fred W. Gretsch.

ALLA TURCA CYMBALS
Turkey

https://soundsanatolian.com/collections/allaturca-turkish-cymbals

Alla Turca Cymbals (Turkey) was founded by Hakan Fidan, one of the previous owners of Pergamon Cymbals.

AMEDIA CYMBALS
Turkey
established 2005

http://www.amediacymbals.com.tr/?lang=en

Ikitelli, Dolapdere Sanayi Sitesi, 13 Ada No: 7-33 Başakşehir, Istanbul / Turkey

+90 212 549 54 76   +90 212 549 04 10

info@amediacymbals.com.tr   www.amediacymbals.com.tr

AMEDIA CYMBALS USA

80 Pompton Ave. Suite 202 Verona, NJ 07044   973-857-5048

Eremya Arzat   Ahmet Baykusak   Saban Baykusak   Hamdusana Baykusak

Eremya Arzat, at age 15, learned the process of cymbal making as an apprentice with "the famous Zilcan" (presumably this means Mikael Zildjian.). According to the Amedia company, almost every present cymbal smith who learned the process in Turkey over the past 28 years learned from Eremya Arzat or one of his apprentices.

Ahmet Baykusak was one of the apprentices of Eremya Arzat and is a co-owner of Amedia Cymbals. He is also the chief hammer smith with fifteen years experience. Ahmet is credited with creating a number of popular cymbal series such as Ahmet Legend, Eremya, Arzat, Komagene, and Old School. Ahmet has control over every cymbal that leaves the factory.

Saban Baykusak is a cousin of Ahmet Baykusak, a partner of the Amedia company, and a master hammer smith.

Hamdusana Baykusak, brother of Ahmet, is a master lathes man with years of experience. He puts the the final touches on each cymbal and applies the logos and stamps.

Mikael Zildjian, upper right,   Eremya Arzat, center right

ANATOLIAN CYMBALS
Turkey
established 1999 https://anatoliancymbals.org/

Anatolian cymbals are hand crafted in Turkey from B20 bronze. Anatolian is run by Temel and Baris Tamdeger (who are nephews of Mehmet Tamdeger - the founder of Istanbul Mehmet cymbals). After co-founding Istanbul Cymbals and working in the factory for years they set up their own foundry, Anatolian, in 1999. Anatolian cymbals are completely hand hammered using traditional methods.

From the website:

Alloy

Anatolian cast bronze cymbals are crafted from the Anatolian B20plus alloy consisting of 80% copper, 20% tin, as well as a secret special additive known only to Anatolian.

Production

Anatolian cymbals are manufactured in our own foundry and production facility. In the first step of the manufacturing process, blanks are cast out of the alloy. This is followed by a complex tempering process. The blanks are rolled over and over again in different directions and heated repeatedly. This involved process causes a change in the molecular structure, which is an important basis for the density, flexibility and durability of the metal. Next, the discs are precisely cut to shape for further processing. The Anatolian cymbal masters, absolute authorities in their field, now begin the time consuming job of hammering the cymbals by hand. After hammering the cymbals, our cymbal masters then lathe them and put the finishing touches to them. During every stage of production the cymbals are subject to constant quality control before going through the final check.

ARBOREA
China
https://arboreacymbal.com/
Fanjia Vililage, Shuizhai Town, Zhangqiu City, Shandong, China
+86-13065067610   arborea@jsycymbals.com

150 Years of Arborea

1864
The founder of "ARBOREA Percussion Instrument" —Fan Xi'an who was 13 years old, worked at Jinan copper percussion instrument factory as an apprentice.

1889
Fan Bingjun the son of Fan xi'an was invited to a famous copper percussion instrument factory which locatedin Zhoucun, Shandong province as a great master.

1909
Fan Xun worked at the percussion department of the Beijing National Musical Instument Factory

1930
Fan Dongwu, Jinan Musical Instrument Factory start trying to make cymbals.

1949
Fan Pixiang inherit the technology of the ancestors, worked at Jinan Musical Instrument Factory as a master.

1986
Fan Guangchun, Zhangqiu Jinshengyuan Musical Instrument Factory was established.

2003 - Now
   Fan Yurong, the current owner of Arborea Cymbal Co.,Ltd took over the production and in the same year cooperated with German company. The export business of copper percussion instruments started.
   Developed new cymbals of each series and the technology of rolling cymbal blank was invented. This improved the cymbal sound fundamentally for the second time.

Most Arborea cymbals are made of B20 bronze which is 80% copper and 20% tin. They also produce B10 and B8 cymbals as well as other alloys and brass cymbals.

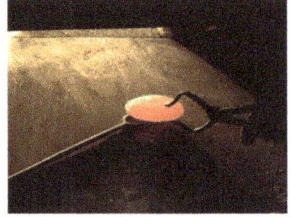

The castings are heated to around 700-800 C in our oven. The heated castings are now soft and ready to go under the rolling machine to become metal discs, or "blanks".

ARTCYMBAL
Japan
https://www.artcymbal.com   yamatake@fa3.so-net.ne.jp

Manabu Yamamoto was born in Tochigi, Japan, in 1988. In 2016, at the age of 27, Manabu began making cymbals as M. Yamamoto Cymbals Japan. At that time he already had been studying and experimenting with music for over 10 years and had collected over 100 vintage cymbals. He built a lathing facility in Tochigi. He began with brass cymbals and reworking existing cast cymbals. After a trip to Turkey in 2018 at the age of 29, Manabu began making cymbals from traditional Turkish B20 bronze and changed the name of his operation to Artcymbal. In May of 2023, the Avedis Zildjian Co. (USA) announced that Yamamoto had joined Zildjian as a Cymbal Innovation Specialist.

In these comments from his website, Manabu points out three of his unique approaches to cymbal construction:

1. The Japanese Tankin method of hammering. "I use a traditional Japanese hammering method, called "TANKIN". Normally, hammering is about thinning the metal, but in TANKIN we can also thicken the metal by hitting it in a certain angle, and gather the bronze to certain areas. It takes a vast amount of time, for example 20 hours of hammering for a 24". This results in unique sounds that I like."

2. The completely hand-formed bell. "I start from a completely flat sheet of B20 bronze which I import from the best foundries in Turkey. (In some YM and YC series I used blanks with a hydraulic pressed cup, which is normal in modern cymbalmaking.) By hand-forming it, it gives a great density to the bell, and opens up bright and complex overtones. Also I often make the bells "off-centered" or not in a perfectly round shape, because it produces the mysterious sound I want. The Istanbul Ks and the original Constantinople Ks gave me the inspiration for the hand-formed bell."

3. Acoustic tuning. "I design my ARTCYMBAL to blend perfectly with unplugged acoustic instruments, even with a unplugged solo violin. Through the past 70 years, general cymbal sounds seems to have become "brighter, louder, and simpler". I want to take you back in time when people enjoyed music without hurting their ears. Every ARTCYMBAL has a wide dynamic range, a wide frequency range, multiple tonal characters to enjoy every moment in music."

Production

ARTISAN TURK
Turkey
https://www.artisanturkcymbals.com/
Founded in 2021 in Turkey by Master Cymbalsmiths
Ertegan Caliskan and Ismet Olcer

from the website

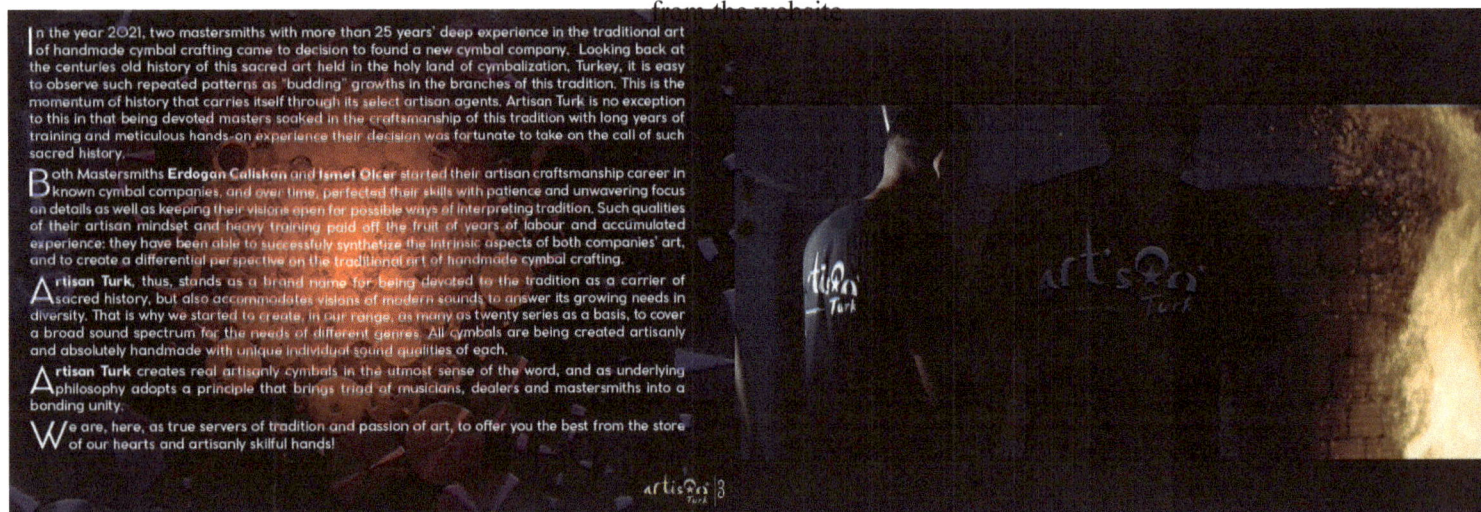

In the year 2021, two mastersmiths with more than 25 years' deep experience in the traditional art of handmade cymbal crafting came to decision to found a new cymbal company. Looking back at the centuries old history of this sacred art held in the holy land of cymbalization, Turkey, it is easy to observe such repeated patterns as "budding" growths in the branches of this tradition. This is the momentum of history that carries itself through its select artisan agents. Artisan Turk is no exception to this in that being devoted masters soaked in the craftsmanship of this tradition with long years of training and meticulous hands-on experience their decision was fortunate to take on the call of such sacred history.

Both Mastersmiths **Erdogan Caliskan** and **Ismet Olcer** started their artisan craftsmanship career in known cymbal companies, and over time, perfected their skills with patience and unwavering focus on details as well as keeping their visions open for possible ways of interpreting tradition. Such qualities of their artisan mindset and heavy training paid off the fruit of years of labour and accumulated experience: they have been able to successfuly synthetize the intrinsic aspects of both companies' art, and to create a differential perspective on the traditional art of handmade cymbal crafting.

Artisan Turk, thus, stands as a brand name for being devoted to the tradition as a carrier of sacred history, but also accommodates visions of modern sounds to answer its growing needs in diversity. That is why we started to create, in our range, as many as twenty series as a basis, to cover a broad sound spectrum for the needs of different genres. All cymbals are being created artisanly and absolutely handmade with unique individual sound qualities of each.

Artisan Turk creates real artisanly cymbals in the utmost sense of the word, and as underlying philosophy adopts a principle that brings triad of musicians, dealers and mastersmiths into a bonding unity.

We are, here, as true servers of tradition and passion of art, to offer you the best from the store of our hearts and artisanly skilful hands!

ASABAG, NETANEL
Israel
https://asabagcymbals.com/

My name is Netanel (Nate) Asabag and I am a cymbal smith from Israel.

As a jazz drummer, the search for the perfect ride cymbal or hi-hats has always piqued my curiosity.

My journey began when I purchased a beautiful, used 22" Avedis ride cymbal, which was wonderful but a bit heavy. Since I couldn't find anyone in Israel who could lathe it for me, I decided to build my own lathe machine. Not long after that, I ordered my first blanks, and since then, I've been on a journey of exploration, learning how to create the best cymbals I can. Cymbal making is a feeling, a mindset, a craft, and an ongoing quest for sonic beauty.

Although I ship worldwide, you are also welcome to visit me at my workshop in Kvutzat Shiller, Center District, Israel. I always have some cymbals in stock and offer a great bop kit and coffee on-site! See you soon.

BERPSON
China
Shanghai, China +234 802 089 2055
jacobsdaniel2010@gmail.com

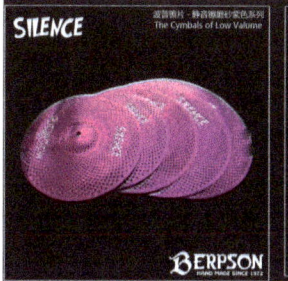

ASHMORE CYMBAL COMPANY
UK
https://www.ashmorecymbals.com/   ryan@ashmorecymbals.com

BFC   Brazilian Finest Cymbals
Brazil
https://bfccymbals.com   contato@bfccymbals.com.br

BFC Brazilian Finest Cymbals is the Brazilian B20 Bronze cymbal brand with 100% Made in Brazil processes. From the foundry (of 80% Copper with 20% Tin, which forms the unbeatable B20 Bronze alloy), to the hammering, concept and development, everything is done in a new way in Brazil with great pride and above all, Finest!

The Brazilian Finest Cymbals are made in a perfect synergy between the artisanal form of the classic Turkish school, adding new technologies and more westernized and modern solutions in its construction.

The manufacture of BFC Dry Dark Cymbals is led by the master cymbalsmith Francisco Domene Nishida, with the expertise and vanguard of Ricardo Goedert from Batera Clube. They joined forces and ideas to create and make BFC Cymbals available to all stores and drummers from Brazil and the world.

The name Brazilian Finest Cymbals was the starting point and inspiration for the birth of this brand. We are inspired by this name to materialize our dreams and desires in the form of cymbals. Our inspiration also comes from the beauty, elegance and fierce that our beautiful and rich music has created and spread around the world. From our sophisticated Bossa Nova and Brazilian Jazz to the fury of Brazilian Rock and Metal, from the groove and swing of our Black Music, our good music is not only Brazilian it is above all Finest. Thus Brazilian Finest Cymbals was born, to be in the hands of the most inspired and inspirational drummers in the world!

Ricardo Goedert and Chico Domene

FRANCISCO DOMENE

Notes from Steve Maxwell interview with Francisco at 2023 Chicago Drum Show:

I have a foundry, so I am in control of the complete process. I select the materials, make the bronze, do the rolling, press bells, I have machine hammering and hand hammering, I was trained by Mustafa Diril in Turkey. I traveled many times to Turkey and am very close to Mustafa. I share the training that I have received, I do not keep secrets. When Mike visited, I took him to the melting room to show him because it is like a cake recipe- you can have the correct ingredients but if you do not do things in the correct order, it does not work.

So when you get a sheet of bronze, then it is when you hammer and work with it that you put your personality into it. And of course what matters the most is the sound- if the sound is correct for you, that is all that matters.

I have been making cymbals since 2000. I was a drummer who knew nothing about this. I had Zildjians and Sabians and B8 crap from Brazil. So I got some bronze and started hammering and ruined many pieces. Then I started buying blanks from Turkey, then wanted to make my own Bronze because I wanted to control everything. The first time I went to Turkey was in 2009, I started the foundry around 2017.

Maxwell: Charcoal, electric, gas, oil- does it make a difference in the way the metal comes out?
Francisco: Yes. We use gas. Oil is messy. Most of the Turkish companies use a wood fire for the rolling and tempering, and bell pressing. We do use gas; it is cleaner but does slightly change the sound. There are a thousand little variables which is why no two cymbals can be identical

When that cymbal goes through the rollers, it's going to achieve a different grain every time depending on which way it goes through the roller. That's why you can get 20 18" medium thin crashes where the manufacturing steps are identical for each and they are all going to sound different. Like wood, there is grain

As a manufacturer, there are some things we cannot control; the grain, the pressure you put on the lathe... you can remove exactly the same amount of material, but you cannot duplicate exactly where. So when you order a cymbal by weight, it does not make sense. This is because the weight may be in different places. For example, a 100 g crash; if 90% of the weight is still in the bell, it will sound different on the edge

Timothy Robert Interview, The Reverie Podcast

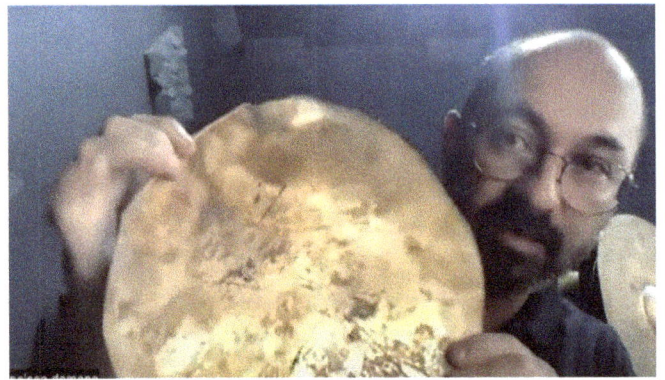

Timothy Roberts interview with Francisco

TR: How did you get to this stage of your cymbal making career?
FD: It started simply because I was curious as to how my cymbals were made. I tried to research this, but could not find detailed information about the process. I knew that hammering was involved, so I tried hammering my cymbals. I soon found that I could easily ruin a cymbal by hammering it. I also soon began to understand how to make acoustic modifications to my cymbals by hammering them, but still I wanted to know more about how the cymbals were manufactured. I knew that many cymbals were being made in Turkey, so I began writing to Turkish cymbal companies. Nobody answered me. Then, finally, I received a message from Amedia that started a dialogue, and led to my first visit to Istanbul in 2009. The visit was rather frustrating, as I witnessed the process but did not understand it. When I left, I took some blanks with me. I simply experimented with the hammering and lathing processes until I finally managed to produce playable cymbals. I continued to use Turkish blanks; I used Amedia, I used Mustafa Diril, I used Masterworks. I lived in Japan for six years where I studied sound engineering at the Yamaha school of music. This helped me to better understand the

FRANCISCO DOMENE

physics of acoustics.

The next step on my journey was when I received a Facebook message from Mustafa Diril, who invited me to visit him in Turkey. I went, and I learned a lot from him. We became very good friends. He came to Brazil to help me build my first factory, with a foundry, in 2017. This was not an easy process. We built the rolling mill, and it broke. We rebuilt it, and it broke again. We eventually figured out how to fix the gears and the transmission. We built up the factory so it was functioning and I was able to hire people. Now we have 38 people working at the factory. We have a foundry, rolling mill, a bell press, presses to press the profile, the rotary hammer, and the machine to trim the edges. I have learned that the most valuable and important component of the factory is the human staff. The people that work with me are my gold. I don't hide any information. You are an artist, Tim, and I am an artist. Here I have artists working in the factory. I cannot help someone who comes here and says they want a Timothy Roberts type cymbal. If you want a Picasso, you cannot have Renoir produce it for you.

Mustafa is a very kind man and has a wonderful family. He has three sons; none of them wanted to follow in his footsteps of crafting cymbals. I am following in his footsteps. I have had many visitors here to the factory; Mike Mongiello, Marcus from Argentina- he was my first student and he is working with me now here. He works here for two months, goes back to Argentina for one month, and comes back here. I learn from him and he learns from me. The knowledge is an exchange; I feel we are all trying to make our own things better and if you look only at what you are doing, it is difficult to improve yourself.

TR: It's true. I've been working on cymbals for about five years, and am still constantly changing my techniques. I will learn something from you or from Paul Frances, begin to use this new technique with the attitude that it will now be what I do every time... then I learn the limitations of that technique, and I am again adjusting... I feel like it is a constant evolution because there is not just one way of making a cymbal. There are traditional Turkish techniques, there are Asian techniques, there is hand hammering, machine hammering, and ways to blend the methods. . there is always going to be this journey, especially since every blank responds differently.

FD: Yes, all blanks are one of a kind, so you need to figure out how to fix the mistakes you did...
When you look at a piece of bronze, you cannot spot the micro things that happen when you start. While you are working with getting your experience from your craft, you start to learn the movement. You can look at the piece and think "Now I need to fix this bump... because later, it will cause this...." It's a matter time, and devotion. You need to hammer a lot of cymbals and make a lot of mistakes to understand. I can't teach you that.

TR: I agree. The way I look at it, you have to find the boundaries. And you cant find the boundaries unless you push against them, unless you explore to the outer reaches. How thin can the cymbal be before it cracks? How tall can it be before it cracks? Or how tall can it be before you hate the sound? You have to find the extremes and from there you can dial it back. You finally start to see the cymbal as if with a microscope, like in another dimension. You can't just say, "I want to make it tall," and focus only on that- the result will lack versatility

FD: I am grabbing a flat blank here. Most people see only a flat blank. I see a lot of things that you cannot see because you do not have the experience that I have. I can see the tiny fissures where the crystals are elongating, you know? The position where I am going to begin hammering is very important, because you will be stretching... The best way to start hammering is to look at all the grains and start where the grain is more elongated. To understand this, you need to understand the blanks, the microstructure, and how bronze "matures". It is common to hear the phrase "The bronze becomes more stiff when it becomes older..." The older the blank, the stiffer the metal. The analogy that I use is to think of sugar, which is also a crystal. You get a jar and put the sugar inside the jar. Shake it- the sugar is very loose. Let it rest for one year. When you then pick up the jar, the sugar is one block. The same things happen with bronze cymbal blanks. The crystals "settle down". Copper wants to be with copper, and tin wants to be with tin. The molecules actually move.

TR: You can feel that. You play a cymbal that was made in the 1960s and it feels so different than a cymbal that was just made...

FD: There is more stick definition..

FRANCISCO DOMENE

TR: It has become more brittle, and that brittleness represents itself as a tighter sound...

FD: Two things that are frequently discussed are stiffness and tension. When I talk about tension, I am talking about tension at the outer edge. The more tension I have on the cymbals, the tighter the edges, so there is less movement. It is different than *stiffness* of the material.

TR Compressing the metal makes it stiffer...

FD Yes. For example, if you press a bell into a blank, it will sound different than if you form the bell by hammering. You have more definition with the pressed bell because the material has many deformations and is thicker. If you create a jazz cymbal with a beautiful "wash" sound and more overtones, you must hammer the bell. The closer to a 90 degree angle between the bell and the body, the more there will be separate sounds from the bell and the body. So if you strike the bell, it sounds like a bell and just a little bit washy on the cymbal. When the slope of the bell is more gradual you can hear more of the "bell area playing" at the edges. You have opened the sound and the wash comes out. These differences can be heard if you have trained your ear to listen for them. You must also learn to hear when a cymbal is finished. Sometimes you should not think about how to fix that bump- it is finished!

TR: How do you know that?

FD: You need to feel it. If you are determined to solve every problem, you will never stop hammering and you will never figure out how to make perfect cymbals.

TR: I am currently trying to make cymbals that have a sort of controlled sense of chaos. Whenever I play a Spizzachino ride, I feel that he intentionally kind of made his cymbals a little chaotic- he wasn't trying to make clean, pristine sounds- in a masterful way he made contained chaos.

FD: Yes, you need to figure out how to control the spectrum. Let's say I want to make two rides, each of which will be one of a kind. We cannot exactly replicate a cymbal. But we can figure out how to control the sustain, the explosion, the tone, the bell, the stick definition,

TR: And you cannot force your expectations on the blank, you have to listen to what the blank is telling you... you have to let go and make this cymbal go, and see what comes out.

I have sourced blanks from Turkey for years, and I always found that the Turkish blanks had a character that was just dark... A darker tone with more imperfections in the metal. That's not to say the imperfections are a bad thing. When I started using your blanks I found that they are much cleaner, the shapes are much more uniform. That has given me more freedom to get dirty or dark sounds if I want to, but I can also get brighter and cleaner sounds than I was ever able to before.

Tell me a little bit about the process in your factory, because it seems that your blanks come out better- I like them more. I don't know why that is.

FD: In the factory, we start with tin and copper. B20 cymbal bronze means 20% tin and 80% copper. When you talk about B8, B12, B15, B20... these are all bronze alloys with different ratios of tin and copper. If you use zinc instead of tin, the resultant alloy is known as brass instead of bronze.

Tin is the most expensive metal in the alloy. Both of these metals are 99.99% pure. The copper does not need to be quite so pure, but the tin must be very pure because if there are traces of lead or aluminum, it will screw the process up. We melt the copper and the tin. We do a metal cleaning process by adding a little carbon to the molten metal. We throw some charcoal and mix everything together to avoid oxygen. We found that oxygen can cause problems in the casting; it can become porous, with lots of little gas bubbles. We grab the crucible, which weighs 75 kilos, put it in the vise, and pour. The person who is pouring needs to know how to pour the right amount of material into pan. If you want a 22" ride, you need an ingot that is 3 1/2 kilo. When they become rigid, we classify each one by weight and let them rest overnight. When they are completely cool, we make visual inspections. If there is a hole caused by a gas bubble, the ingot is failed. Before every drop of an ingot, we need to clean the pan to avoid problems in the rolling mill. If there is an imperfection, that ingot needs to be remelted and cast again. When the ingots are approved and cleaned, then they go to the next process which is the rolling mill. There is a huge oven that heats the ingots to 750 degress celcius (1380 F). At that temperature, the ingot becomes cherry red. It goes into the rolling mill which stretches the grains and flattens the ingot. Then it goes back to the oven, and again into the rolling mill, this time rotated 90 degrees. This results in a cross-structure of the crystals.

As we repeat the process of reheating and rolling the blank many times, a black crust layer is formed on the top. We have a choice; we can leave the oxidation or we can remove it before the next step which heat treatment or quenching. Why would we remove the black crust? The oxidation is like a blanket that will mute the sound. If you leave it, you will have a blackish blank that will sound more dry. To remove the oxidation, we wash it with salt before the heat treatment. This produces a brighter-colored blank

TR: I have had both kinds of blanks. The ones with the oxidation still on them really dull the lathe bits much more quickly.

FD: B20 cymbal bronze goes through phases. In each phase, the metal has certain physical properties. When the blank is at the stage we have just explained, after it has been heated and rolled many times, it is very brittle. If you drop it, it will shatter like glass and you can even break it with your bare hands. The phase that I need for my blanks is when the metal is malleable. Also there needs to be some "spring" response so it will come back to the initial shape. How do we change from the brittle phase to the malleable phase and then "lock it in" at that phase? This is done with heat treatments. We say heat treatments because tempering in incorrect- it is heat treatment and quenching. This means heating the blank to a certain temperature in the oven, then plunging it into water to cool it. This is called quenching, and is often done with salt water. There is another variable to consider at this stage, and that is the temperature window of the "freeze temperature". If I go too high on the temperature, the cymbal becomes more malleable and the pitch it produces becomes more low. If I lower the temperature used during the quenching, then the pitch becomes more high.

Another variable is the amount of time it stays in the oven. For example, I am using propane gas in my oven. (I burn a great deal of propane gas in my factory!) The way that the gas flames arrive on the cymbal will react with the cymbal. If the angle, proximity, or intensity of the flames are changed, the sound will change. The temperature can be the same, but the way that the flames approach the cymbal can change the sound.

So, to quickly review the variables to this point: We have the option of a salt cleaning or no salt cleaning, we have the temperature before quenching it in the water, and we have the location in the oven where the cymbal is placed. At the top of the oven we have more efficient heat from the bricks because it is reflective. So if the cymbals are higher in the oven, they will be heated faster

TR: I think of all of these stages from melting the metals through quenching the plates as the "back end" of the production process, and the stages of hammering and lathing as the "front end". There are many things you we can do on the back end to change the sound of the cymbal, there are also many things on the front end to change what the sound possibilities are.

FD: Oh yes, And here are some more "back end" variables. If you use a charcoal and wood fire, you need to put the charcoal on the floor- it makes an insulation from the bricks. It's very different when you use charcoal than when you use electrical or gas- these are all different methods.

TR: Let's talk a little about tension. This would be one of the "phases" you mentioned. This phase reminds me of a guitar string. When the string is loose, there is no tension on it and there is no sound because the string cannot vibrate. It is the tension that allows the cymbal to have a sustaining note or tone.

FD: The physical properties of the metals in the alloy are important. The more you hammer copper, the stiffer it becomes. You can hammer copper to increase the tension, then rehammer to further increase tension, and on and on. With B20, you hammer not only to change the tension, but also the shape. When the shape is changed, you cannot "back up" if you went too far, you must start over. You can do tension relief with fire on B20, but you need to understand what you are doing. Otherwise you have screwed everything and it becomes brittle again.

B20, B21, B22, B18, B19, whatever... they are *all* different metals. There are physical properties that belong only to each alloy. If you grab a cymbal made from a B8 blank and you are a monster drummer using a 2B stick and to hit the cymbal with all of your force, you may change the shape of the cymbal permanently- it is deformed. It is holding the excessive pressure. If you do the same thing with a B20 cymbal, it will break. B8

FRANCISCO DOMENE

tends to crack less than B20. Which is the best one? It depends. Both metals have their own properties. The drummer wants the best sound for his own purpose. There are of course differences between different B8 cymbals. The metal is the same, but the amount of work on the cymbal will make the entire difference in sound.

TR: Paiste, for example, has for a long time made B8 cymbals that sound great, while for many other brands, B8 is their entry-level cymbal.

FD: Let's return to my process for making cymbals. We have cast the ingot, heated and rolled it, then heat treated and quenched it. Now we have a blank that is not perfectly round and does not have a bell or a center hole. We drill a hole in the center, and we cut the blank so it is round. Then we can create the profile.

You can create a profile by pressing or by hammering. Think of a steel drum with different notes. When a cymbal blank is pressed into a profile, the tone remains purer. When you hammer a blank into a profile, each hammer strike adds to the complexity of the sound. More pitches are added, until ultimately you have white noise, a combination of all pitches.

TR: So with a hammered profile, you can get...

FD: More highs. Let's talk a little bit about sound waves. High frequencies are very short sound waves with much less energy than the biggest low frequencies. If there are little bumps (from hammering), they disrupt the longer (lower) waves.

Right now we have profile dyes for high hats, the crashes, and rides, all with almost the same profile.

TR: And you can press just a small amount of profile, so the finished profile is accomplished with hammering?

FD: Yes, that is very easy to control.

TR: I suppose most of the larger companies are pressing most profiles, while smaller Turkish companies are swinging the hammers..

FD: There is a trend with the Turkish makers toward more machine hammering. It is simply more cost-effective to produce faster and with less human labor. More human labor means more training, and more of everything that goes with having more employees.

TR: Has this transition started quite recently?

FD: No, it has been a while. To be clear, they are all still making great cymbals. If you want a Turkish sound, you must buy blanks from Turkey, or buy cymbals from Turkey. The charcoal, the marks...

TR: I find that I can still, with your blanks, add complexity and darkness, etc. with my own processes. There is fundamentally a different baseline for me. I'm sure the charcoal and wood fires and other processes introduce imperfections, is that true?

FD: Yes, I have a cleaner process. My process is not better, but it is different.

Matt Bettis Interview

MATT BETTIS
USA
http://bettiscymbals.com matt@bettiscymbals.com

Q - Are you still making cymbals?
A - Yes. After making over 3,000 cymbals, I have slowed down my production. However, I still make cymbals for a select list of clients.

BIG ISLAND CYMBALS
USA

Russell Lundgren
www.bigislandcymbals.com

Hawaii's First and Original Cymbalsmith. Creating cymbals inspired by nature and the beauty of Hawaii. Hand crafted and hammered. Mahalo For Looking!

Borba Cymbals
USA
https://www.borbacymbals.com

Officially launched in April 2021, Borba Cymbals is a one man, independent cymbal crafting operation. Founder Brett Borba transforms Turkish B20 bronze blanks into high quality instruments in his small workshop in sunny California.

Production

BOSPHORUS CYMBALS
Turkey
https://www.bosphoruscymbals.com/

Bosphorus Cymbals was established in 1996 by three master cymbal smiths who were formerly with the Istanbul cymbal company; Hasan Seker, Ibrahim Yakici and Hasan Ozdemir. They are called Masters because they are the most experienced cymbal smiths in Turkey who are still working actively.

Mattia Bourgis
Spain
https://mbcymbals.com/

The MATTIA BOURGIS Cymbals are 100% hand made from highest quality Turkish b20 blanks.
All these cymbals are music instruments of higher level, all are unique pieces hammered and crafted in the old good style to deliver a dark, rich and vivid sound.

Who I am

I'm a jazz drummer with a diploma in classical music with experiences in several styles of music.
I've been playing classical music in orchestras, hard-rock ACDC tribute band, soul & rythm blues, progressive rock, afro-beat, green music, Italian traditional music.

BRASSWOOD
Netherlands
https://www.facebook.com/Brasswooddrums

Marius Buck
Germany
http://buckblech.de/ info@buckblech.de
Großherzog-Friedrich-Strasse 95, 66111 Saarbrucken
Mobile: 0151/28491898

Buffalo Cymbals
USA
www.buffalocymbalsmiths.com
Thomas Foote

cymbals from bronze blanks, repurposing broken cymbals into playable art. Jewelry and metalsmithing #BuffaloCymbalsmiths

BURKE DAUGHERTY

https://www.bronzepie.com/

My search for the perfect Jazz ride is what ultimately led to the creation of Bronze Pie. Years ago, I spent many hours lurking around on Cymbalholic.com reading post by and about cymbalsmiths such as Craig Laurenston, Robert Spizzichino, Matt Bettis, Mike Skiba and Matt Nolan, I was trying to learn as much as possible about what was involved in making superb cymbals. That site was wonderful, between the knowledgeable players, enthusiast and cymbalsmiths it was pure inspiration to me. I set out on modifying cymbals, for better and worse, some down right tortured in the quest for fundamental cymbal knowledge. Then to hammering some stainless steel because it's so readily available. Yeah, I wanted an old Zildjian K, but couldn't justify the cost. Next up was a cymbal made by Robert Spizzichino, then he passed away RIP, so that put his cymbals out of reach. I do admit to cymbal snobbery here. Acquiring those two cymbals were what kept me up at night, and admittedly overlooking the wonderful cymbals being made by todays best cymbalsmiths. I eventually purchased two wonderful Matt Bettis cymbals and that cured my obsession for a handmade cymbal for a while...the term cymbalholic will resonate with those that have the condition. The horizon just moved further away.

RAY BYRNE

https://byrnecymbals.com/

Ray Byrne has been making cymbals under the brand Byrne Cymbals since 2016. As an alumnus of The Roberto-Venn School of Lutherie Ray already had an extensive background in instrument building and repair. Drumset was always his first passion but when it came to instrument building the process of cymbal-making always seemed so elusive. However, after years of experimenting and research, Ray was finally able to take the first steps towards cymbal smithing after watching the well-known Spizzichino mini-documentary which opened the door of possibility. Ray's business approach focuses on making small batches of custom orders for a curated clientele, and working with select drum shops.

Ray likes to think of his cymbal crafting procedures in terms of stages: he works with the bigger hammers first, then smaller hammers, and lets the cymbal rest for at least a day. If he is shipping a specially crafted cymbal for a discerning customer, he will age it for a month, checking it weekly.

Ray feels that a good balance between stick and wash is important. He also feels that all cymbals are, in a sense, wearing out. Like a prewar Martin guitar, a cymbal can open up continually until it is finally "played out".

When asked for his opinion on cymbal cleaning, he points out that this is a somewhat controversial topic. His own preference is to let a cymbal age and develop it's own patina. An exception would be the development of the "green stuff" which should probably be removed. To force a patina, Ray suggests a mixture of Miracle Grow and vinegar.

ARIEL CALABRIA
USA

1617 Groves Ave NW, Olympia, WA,
(360) 797-4034 arielcee@yahoo.com
https://www.facebook.com/indipendantcymbals

I hand hammer and lathe custom cymbals made from high quality Turkish blanks.

LANCE CAMPEAU
Canada

thecymbalproject@hotmail.com   https://www.youtube.com/user/LanceCampeau

The Cymbal Project™ is a video series by Lance Campeau that shows how to repair and modify cymbals.
The Cymbal Project™ video series covers topics such as…
- Cymbal repair & refurbishment (cutting & resizing)
- Cymbal cleaning (chemical polishing, abrasive polishing)
- Cymbal modification (re-hammering, lathing, patina treatment)
- Cymbal-smithing techniques (hammering & shaping)
- How to source inexpensive cymbals for experimentation
- How to make cymbal-smithing tools (hammers, anvils, lathe)
- Making custom cymbals from sheet metals (steel, brass, etc...)
- Experiments in forging & casting custom cymbal alloys

Custom cymbals are available for sale
https://reverb.com/shop/TheCymbalProject

ALEXINA CECH
Austria

https://www.alexinocymbals.com/

I got born in August 1990 and play the drums since the age of 3. I studied with some of the finest musicians from Europe such as Klemens Marktl, Mario Gonzi,Vladimir Kostadinovic,Roberto Gatto,Dusan Novakov.
I'm working as a sidemen as well as leading my own projects. (Artist page comin soon..)

The underlying assumption is that the fundamental purpose of human existence is to promote happiness, elevate spirits, and act as a force for good, regardless of any specific rationale. This is the guiding principle that informs my actions in my roles as a musician, a cymbal maker, and as a human being in general.

In 2018 I got myself involved in cymbal making, having literally no clue about anything ,but this sound in the ears, which i wanted to accomplish once the cymbal is done.

Prior to embarking on this craft, I had always fantasized about an Old Zildjian K Istanbul Old Stamp with a wooden stick definition and a wash underneath. This combination was distinctly audible but never exceeded the limits of the stick, as we all appreciate from Elvin, Tony, Max, Art Blakey, Mel Lewis, and Philly Joe, among others.

Consequently, I was aware of the desired outcome and embarked on the journey to achieve it.

I did not receive any instruction in cymbal technique from any source, at the time I began crafting those instruments.

The process involved a great deal of trial and error, as well as an understanding of the cause and effect relationships involved. The aim was to identify the sound desired and to develop the ability to create cymbals that would meet the specific requirements of the customer.

My techniques encompass Japanese "Tankin" techniques and a number of techniques that I have developed and discovered through my own research and experimentation. Meanwhile, the process was driven to perfection.

In the case of custom orders, it is of the utmost importance to have a clear understanding of the required process. There is no room for allowing the material to dictate the outcome; rather, it is essential to have a well-defined plan of action.

The comprehension of causality, consciousness, and technical abilities provides the freedom to create without any limitations.

CENTENT

https://www.cententcymbalsusa.com/
sales@cententcymbalsusa.com
803-365-5218

From the Centent website: Legend has it, that one of last remaining dragons helped cast the first bronze cymbal over 4000 years ago in Shandong Province. This way the spirit of the dragon would remain intact, past on through the fires of each forging. Today, Centent Cymbals offers hand crafted, high quality Chinese cymbals. At Centent Cymbals, we take great pride in producing a cymbal that is both a visual work of art and sounds as good as brands costing 2-3 times as much. Unleash the legend once again and find out for your self what makes Centent Cymbals so special.

Centent Cymbals USA offers the highest quality of B8, B10 and B20 bronze cymbals at an amazing value. With the companies roots tracing back almost 400 years to the Qing Dynasty, Centent Cymbals brings generations of traditional craftsmanship and mates that with today's technical advancements. Our modern business approach offers competitive pricing and amazing support to drummers of all levels.

photos courtesy of Arthur Stonez
According to Stonez, a cretical part of the Centent casting process involves the addition of water

Champion Cymbals
New Zealand
https://championcymbals.com/
https://www.instagram.com/championcymbals

DAVE COLLINGWOOD

I'm Dave Collingwood, a full-time independent cymbalsmith based in Bristol, south west UK. At 31 my first child arrived, and I decided to stop touring. I'd heard that making cymbals by hand was a possibility, and read all I could about the masters of the time - some sadly no longer with us. The mixture of creativity and practicality appealed, and I decided it was something I was going to do. Something I HAD to do.

With whatever information was available at the time, I started preparing tools and sourcing material. I decided I was going to learn this craft the hard way - 100% self-taught through trial-and-error. A decision I sometimes (almost) regret - I wasn't ready for the steep learning curve and counter-intuitive nature of some of the processes involved. I persevered, making mistake after mistake, determined to figure out where I'd gone wrong, and how to make it right.

I make cymbals because I can't not make cymbals. It's a passion and an obsession. The more I learn about it, the more I see there is to learn. I'm forever challenging myself to find new techniques and uncover new processes, and with more and more people showing an interest in the craft, I've decided to pass on my knowledge by teaching others how to find their own way through the ever-branching pathways of knowledge.

https://www.collingwoodcymbals.com/

Dave Collingwood Cymbalsmith Training

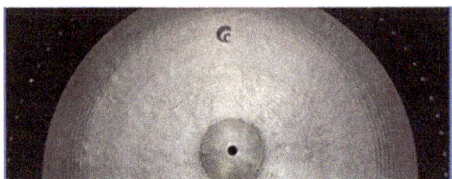

Welcome to the Cymbal Community!
$7 / month

Join

- Welcome, and thank you!
- Join monthly group Zoom meetings with cymbalsmiths from around the world, experienced and newbie alike! You don't have to be a maker - cymbal lovers are most welcome! This is a resource for all to come together in appreciation of these fine instruments.
- Guest content.
- Exclusive posts, videos, tutorials and insights.
- Twice monthly listening party zoning in on cymbal sounds and players. Songs are chosen by you!
- My eternal gratitude.
- Group Zoom Meetings
- Exclusive Content
- Guest Content
- Twice Monthly Listening Party

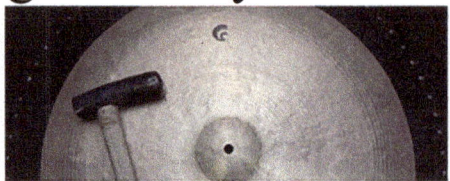

Cymbalsmith Training 1
$16 / month

Join

- Every 6 weeks, 30 minute one-to-one video chat working on your skills as a cymbalsmith.
- Join monthly group Zoom meetings with cymbalsmiths from around the world, experienced and newbie alike!
- Exclusive posts, videos, tutorials and insights.
- Twice monthly listening party zoning in on cymbal sounds and players. Songs are chosen by you!
- My eternal gratitude.
- Cymbalsmith Training
- Group Zoom Meetings
- Exclusive Content
- Guest Content
- Twice Monthly Listening Party

Cymbalsmith Training 2
$26.50 / month

Join

- **Upgrade** to **monthly** 30 minute one-to-one video chat to cover anything you'd like to discuss about making cymbals, making the tools you need & how to approach the metal.
- Join monthly group Zoom meetings with cymbalsmiths from around the world, experienced and newbie alike!
- Exclusive posts, videos, tutorials and insights.
- Twice monthly listening party zoning in on cymbal sounds and players. Songs are chosen by you!
- My eternal gratitude.
- **Exclusive** CC design mug sent after 3 months of patronage!
- Cymbalsmith Training
- Group Zoom Meetings
- Exclusive Content
- Guest Content
- Twice Monthly Listening Party

Show less ∧

Constantine
Turkey
https://www.constantinecymbals-usa.com/about-us

Master cymbalsmith Sertan Oztopuz crafts each of these instruments by hand in Istanbul, Turkey. Sertan spent 32 years at Istanbul (both Agop and Mehmet after the split) where he was trained and eventually taught the use of the coveted Turkish B20 alloy. Constantine recently introduced a line of B25 cymbals, made possible by the skillset of Sertan Oztopuz.

CYMBAL AND GONG
Office in USA, Production in Turkey
https://www.cymbalandgong.com

from the website:

Cymbal & Gong is a one man operation here in Portland-- a drummer named Tim Ennis. Revival was the first place that sold them-- they might have helped out a little bit financially in the beginning.

The smiths are in Istanbul; the main guy previously worked for one of the major brands, and they have their own excellent brand that is different from C&G.

CYMATIC CYMBALS
USA
https://www.instagram.com/cymatic_cymbals/#

PAUL FRANCIS

paul@cymbalcraftsman.com

Paul Francis, from Quincy, MA. started playing a snare drum at the age of 10, then got his first drum set when he was 11. He took private lessons on the set until he was 28.

Paul attended Berklee College of Music in 1986-1987 and later completed the Drummers Collective 10-week certificate program in 1998.

Paul started working for a major cymbal maker in 1988 and was there for 32 years. Over the course of those 32 years, Paul designed many of the cymbals that drummers play today. Paul worked together with Armand Zildjian (who taught him proper cymbal sounds and cymbal designs) on designing the K Constantinople's, A. Zildjian & Cie Vintage series, and 21" Sweet ride among others.
Other mentors included Lennie DiMuzio and Leon Chiappini.

Paul has worked with countless artists on their cymbal sounds and cymbal designs, among them Elvin Jones, Tony Williams, Louie Bellson, Steve Gadd, Bill Stewart, Adam Nussbaum, Peter Erskine, and Steve Smith/

CYMBAL CRAFTSMAN/Royal Cymbals
Paul Francis

comments excerpted from interview at 2023 Chicago Drum Show:

I like to speak about sound... When a cymbal speaks to you as a player and feels right, it makes the other musicians sound better.

We are all using the same type of material. There is the material, the cup shape, the hammering.... There are only two ways to hammer a cymbal; You can have hammer marks in rows or they can be scattered all around... The biggest common theme of my years of making cymbals is that you want a cymbal that can do all things- you want something with good stick definition, but also you can crash. One of the things that Armand Zildjian taught me was that every cymbal is a crash ride. You should be able to ride on every cymbal, you should be able to crash. I'm going to use Adam as an example because I've been working with Adam for 30+ years (points to Adam Nussbaum), Adam likes cymbals that when you shank them they give you a higher note. All of these things come together to give a drummer a signature sound. I think it's kind of funny much discussion there is about certain cymbals- the cymbals do not make any sound until the drummer brings an individual personality to them. To me, it's all about you choosing the sound

When making a batch of cymbals that are all the same size and style, each may quench a little differently. There are differences in thickness and hardness. Don't order blanks and let them sit around for a month, because then you are fighting with the metal. Someone contacted me about doing something with some blanks that they had and I asked how old they are; he said three years. I said nope, I'm not even going to try to hammer those into shape.

Q: how much will a cymbal change in sound over the years?
With a brand new cymbal you can get about 90% there. What happens with the metal is it age hardens over time.
80-20 when it's rolled is like glass- drop it on the floor and it will shatter. So you anneal it and then quench it down, you hammer it and lathe it.... With the hammering, you are putting the strength back into the blank but you had to soften it down in order to put the strengh back into the blank. In the first 48 hours is the biggest change in sound. If you were to hear a cymbal right off of the lathe, you would probably would not play it. It's dull. So in the first 48 hours it starts to to open up as stress is relieved and then slowly over time the metal gets harder. Older cymbals are easier to play because you don't have to put as much energy into them. I have taken really old cymbals and have made duplicates and over time they will start to resemble the original.

At this show we are debuting a brighter sound with the Royal cymbals. For legal reasons the Royal thing couldn't happen until this year. So Cymbal Craftsman is kind of your darker, more complex random hammered cymbal.

CYMBALATELIER
Singapore
https://www.instagram.com/cymbalatelier/#
Cymbals hand made with Turkish B20 Bronze

CYMBALUTOPIA /CRAIG LAURITSON
Australia
http://www.cymbalutopia.com
sales@cymbalutopia.com or eargasmm@ozemail.com.au
My youtube channel - https://www.youtube.com/c/CraigLauritsen
Facebook - https://www.facebook.com/craig.lauritsen
Instagram - https://www.instagram.com/cymbalutop

from website:

Cymbalsmithing and playing drums are my 2 passions. I've been a professional musician for more than thirty years and my obsession with cymbal sounds began soon afterwards.

Some time ago I began a quest to find the 'perfect' cymbal and this passion led to countless hours searching for as much information as I could about all aspects of cymbal creation. Part of my study included getting my hands on many hundreds of cymbals from almost all of the major manufacturers and many independent cymbalsmiths. I studied cymbal weights, profiles, tapers, hammering and lathing techniques, chemical composition, sonic characteristics etc. I also travelled to many different countries, seeking out cymbal makers and master cymbalsmiths. I applied this knowledge to perform my own hammering, lathing and surface treatment techniques to existing cymbals, all in the desire to create more musical pieces of bronze.

When I first started out, I practiced hammering for between an average of 15 - 20 hrs per week for 2 years. I currently spend an average of about 30 - 35 hrs a week cymbalsmithing and I still experiment as much as possible with modifying tools, and new hammering and lathing techniques, continually searching for new sounds and new possibilities.

I use a number of tools and techniques which are completely unique to myself and which impart subtle unique qualities to the sonic characteristics of my cymbals. I've always been attracted to pursuits which reflect subtle differences which can only be attributed to individual input or unquantifiable differences between other factors. For example, I love cooking, coffee, red wine, art, film, literature etc.

Cymbalsmithing is certainly one of those pursuits, a craft where the individual imparts something unique into the final product.

DEFIANT CYMBAL CO.
Office in Mexico, Manufacturing in Turkey
Blvd. García de León 1775, Chapultepec Oriente.,
Morelia Centro, Mexico, 58280
defiantcymbalco@gmail.com
https://www.facebook.com/defiantcymbalcompany/about

HELGE DICHANZ
Netherlands
https://www.youtube.com/@handmodifiedcymbals   jazzitup@web.de
Helge Dichanz is a freelance drummer and cymbal modifier based in Europe.

DIRIL CYMBALS
Ibrahim Diril   Turkey
http://dirilcymbals.com/home-diril-cymbals.html

Ibrahim Diril moved from his home town of Samsun with his parents, brother, and cousins in 1987. He worked for Mehmet and Agop (Istanbul Cymbals) for five years. He then left Istanbul to return to Samsun and work with his brother Murat Diril and cousin Mustafa Diril who had also been trained by Mehmet and Agop. Together they worked with Meinl (creating and producing the Byzance series of cymbals) and Paiste (making the Twenty Series). In 2008, Ibrahim struck out on his own, starting the Diril Cymbals company.

from the Diril Cymbals website:

Our cymbals are all hand made and hand hammered and we use B-20 metal. Ever since the company has been established, our unchanged principle is to maintain a high quality and let the drummers all over the world play our cymbals with great pleasure and joy. Thanks to all the users that it has been the case. In additon to high quality we also offer good prices so that people who doesn't have to pay a fortune for cymbal produced by the big names. Now they are happy and sale figures proves that our cymbals are being appreciated by a large number of drummers.

Making cymbal is a passion for us. It will remain being like that. We will continue making them by hand and we do not approve using machines for that. Cymbal making is an art and machines should not be used to destroy it.

MURAT DIRIL
Turkey

Murat's Story

https://www.muratdiril.com/home.html
Murat Diril began his career at the age of 14 in 1988 working under Mehmet Tamdeger and Agop Tomurcuk in the Istanbul factory. He left Istanbul in 1996 and in 2010 introduced his own brand to the U.S. market. His cymbals are made with a B27 alloy.

ADEM DIRIL
see Mehteran

MUSTAFA DIRIL
see Samsun cymbals

DREAM Cymbals & Gongs
Office in Canada, Manufacturing in China
616-R St. Clarens Ave. Toronto, ON CANADA M6H 3W9
1-877-933-7629
https://dreamcymbals.com/   info@dreamcymbals.com

EMJMD
Japan
https://www.emjmod.com/

Yuuki Emmeiji or "emj" is an artist from Osaka that has collaborated with Koide Cymbals to create cymbal designs that are contemporary expressions in the art of modern cymbal making and modifying.

He is a cymbal lover who owns more than 100 cymbals, and has been independently researching cymbal processing, production, and repair for many years. His activities led to the establishment of the cymbal manufacturer "emjmod". He purchases his own materials and does all the specialized work such as hammering and raising by himself. The cymbals that he makes by hand one by one are unique in both design and tone, but they are handled by major musical instrument stores and are loved by Japan's top drummers and percussionists as "usable tones".

MIKE ERNST CYMBALS
USA
https://mikeernstcymbals.godaddysites.com/   mike@mikeernstcymbals.com

With over 40 years of drumming, I have developed a passion for cymbals. The right cymbal for the application is just as important as a synth or guitar tone, quite simply, it makes the music. How it sounds, plays, and breathes becomes an integral part of the musicality expressed by the drummer.

A love of cymbals and a lifetime of mechanical experience have combined into a passion for sound. Hammering and lathing, breathing new life into broken cymbals and making in tact cymbals come alive.

FUNCH CYMBALS
Denmark
funchcymbals.com

Lasse Funch Furberg

Lasse was educated as a jazz drummer at the Danish National Academy of Music. Sparked by his interest in cymbals, he became a cymbal smith and founded Funch Cymbals in 2017. Lasse studied the Turkish cymbal making tradition in Istanbul. That is the foundation of his cymbal production today. His approach to cymbal making is a fusion of his background as a jazz drummer and the Turkish techniques. His goal is to create cymbals that are highly useable in acoustic jazz settings. As a musician and a craftsman, he is inspired by the jazz history from the early '60s.

"As a drummer I am familiar with the quest for a sound that's just right for me. Years of playing has tuned my ear to know exactly what to listen out for. I pour this knowledge and intuition into each and every cymbal I make. The result is a highly musical instrument of supreme quality." - Lasse

Funch cymbals are inspired by Old Ks. The ones that jazz giants of the past cherished and revered for their organic musicality. The ones that keep you coming back to discover evernew sounds, colors and textures to be drawn out of a single instrument like magic. The ones that remain highly sought after by drummers and musicians around the world to this very day. In essence, all Funch cymblas are a tribute to the Old Ks. Each one has its own unique story to tell and are designed to help you express your originality in the studio or on stage. Here is an overview of our other regularly released collections:

Vanguard - This highly versatile series is clean, warm and buttery with a woody stick sound. They provide a comfortable cushion for the music that would be just as welcomed in small ensembles and intimate clubs as they would be in big bands and theatres. Swing your heart out on these sweet cymbals inspired by Mel Lewis and The Vanguard Jazz Orchestra. This series is produced in all of our standard sizes.

Messenger - These cymbals have the vibes and demeanor that any old school, hard-swingin' cat would kill for. Each one posses a clean stick and strong dark crash, but beyond that it's all about the intangibles and the fact that each one can be characterized by its bold individuality. These are intended to be adaptable workhorse instruments with aspirations of setting the club on fire night after night. They're named after Art Blakey's legendary institution The Jazz Messengers. These cymbals are produced in all of our standard sizes.

Perceptual - These cymbals have a clear and well articulated stick definition buoyed by an even clearer, deep, low-pitched resonance. Their wide bell is integrated into a flatter profile which produces a gorgeous dark shimmer. They are always responsive in a full dynamic range and ready to shine in any circumstance. These are typically produced as 22" and 24", and sometimes have rivets and sometimes do not.

Nefertiti - Named after the iconic and influential album by Miles Davis with the great Tony Williams (TW) on drums. These cymbals are hard-hammered with a medium-high profile and finished with pinstripe lathing. This process gives each cymbal an exotic surface that accentuates its complex shimmer. They are known for their dynamic sensitivity as well as huge spread of active top end and fiery, low growl. All these qualities are complimented by a nice, bright stick sound. Nefertiti's are produced in all of our standard sizes, typically without rivets.

TW Tribute - This series is closely related to Nefertiti - The main difference is that TWs have more top tension. This technique creates a slightly lower profile than Nefertiti and an icy stick sound that is a little bit brighter. The overall character is more complex. They are highly sensitive with a great dynamic range and a fat trashy crash!

Elvin Jones Tribute - Our tributes to Elvin focus on his 20" sounds from the 1960s. To us that means its wash provides a perfectly balanced, sweet and dark cushion for a bright stick attack to dance on. It has a well pronounced bell that cuts, but is not harsh, making it ideal for afro-latin patterns. It has an explosive full-bodied crash with a fast decay. These almost always come with 3 evenly spaced rivets in a triangle pattern that blend in gently to help create that quintessential smokey jazz sizzle.

Flat Rides - Flat rides get their name because they have no bell. Without a bell a cymbal will not be able to project as loudly or buildup hardly any overtones or sustain so what you hear foremost is a whole lot of clicky stick attack. Lasse aims to give their highly controlled wash a dark and throaty character that can be semi-crashable (more like accent-able).

6th Anniversary - This series has completely hand-formed bells, meaning each one is highly individual in its shape, appearance and size just like the old Ks. Overall these rides are low pitched and sound very full and rich. They are dark and washy with a beautiful deep crash and a clean stick.

7th Anniversary - These rides are quite dry with an incredibly clear stick that refuses to wash out no matter how hard you're cookin'. Big fat, soft and shallow hammer strokes and a beautiful patina give this series a truly striking appearance.

GM DESIGNS CYMBALS
USA
https://gmdcymbals.com/

FRANK GEGERLE
Germany
https://www.hieber-lindberg.de/blog/Frank-Gegerle-Cymbals-Ein-einzigartiger-Sound

GIO CYMBALS
Office in USA, Manufactured in Turkey
https://giocymbals.com/   Hi@GIOCymbals.com
(480)242-8213

ALESSANDRO GIOIELLO
Italy
gioiellocymbals@gmail.com
Jazzy handmade cymbals from Turin, Italy (Turkish B20)
(b20 Turkish bronze)

GODEC CYMBALS
Slovenia
https://www.instagram.com/godec_cymbals
Hi, my name is Domen and I'm located in Slovenia. I have started learning the craft of cymbalsmithing a year ago and I am sharing the journey here.

HAYDEN CYMBALS
USA
https://www.haydencustomcymbals.com/

Ryan Hayden is an independent cymbalsmith residing in Denver, Colorado. Each cymbal is made from a B20 Turkish blank that is shaped on an anvil, then lathed to completion. Ryan is a current student of Dave Collingwood (Collingwood Cymbals) and has studied with Timothy Roberts (Timothy Roberts Cymbals).

As a professional drummer who has received a BM for Berklee College of Music and an MM from The Juilliard School, he brings his professional experience and knowledge of music into handcrafting each cymbal.

HEAD CUSTOM CYMBALS
Italy
Thomas Head Testa, Numana, Italy
https://www.facebook.com/headcustomdrumsandcymbals/
headcustomcymbals@gmail.com   +39 342 645 2616

HEARTBEAT PERCUSSION
Office in Canada, Manufactured in Turkey
#104 9775 188 Street, Surrey, BC, Canada V4N 3N2
Toll Free: 866.988.1277 Local: 604.888.1277
https://www.heartbeatpercussion.com/   info@heartbeatpercussion.com

A boutique company established in 2003, Heartbeat Percussion features high quality products made available at affordable prices. Cymbals, drums, bags, sticks and hardware are part of the growing Heartbeat Percussion family.

HERSHKO CYMBALS
Israel
https://www.hershcocymbals.com/
https://www.instagram.com/hershkocymbals/#
Hand crafted Cymbals, made by Cymbalsmith Ron Hershkovitz,
DM or email hershkocymbals@gmail.com for inquiries.

HOMEMADE CYMBALS
Germany
http://www.homemadecymbals.com/

STEVE HUBBACK
Netherlands
https://www.stevehubback.nl
gongmaker2000@yahoo.com

Biography

Steve is from Barry in South Wales where his musical career began in 1978 playing in local rock and rock and roll groups and later attending the Barry Jazz and Improvised music Summer School where he met and was inspired by Tony Oxley. Gordon Beck. Evan Parker. Alan Holdsworth. Phil Wachsman. Trevor Tomkins. Roy Babington. Keith Tippet. Alan Skidmore. Fred Van Hove, Peter Brotzmann and many other great musicians. It was a life changing experience.

He started a jazz club in Barry in a big hotel which became well known in Wales and soon after a Friday night rock club in the same venue. After turning professional Steve left Wales for Paris in early 1981 which was a fantastic cultural and learning experience. During his time in Paris he first played in a rock 'n' roll group and later in the rock group Splat with Goffo and Joe Hamilton.. He also began performing solo and performed surrealist theater with Italian Artist – dancer/sculptor Loredana Celi. Steve learnt a lot from Loredana about working with visual and movement. In 1983 Steve also had the opportunity to perform in Versailles with the legendary Bob Vatel.

In Paris in 1985 Steve founded It's My Head with guitarist 'Goffo' from London. Music with powerful atmospheres of industrial energy combined with surrealistic explorations with moments of intense beauty. It's My Head toured in Denmark. Norway and Sweden. Goffo left in 1986 and Steve invited the phenomenal Swedish guitarist Jorgen Cremonese from Kai Martin og Stick to join the band. The highly acclaimed debut LP was recorded in Aarhus with Danish guitarist R L Lunding from the band Picnic and at Jorgen Sangsta's Urania Studios in Gothenburg Sweden with Jorgen Sangsta contributing a rythym track on Mime For The Blind. Steve played drums, motorized guitar, keyboards and made recordings of live smashing glass and metal sheets dropped from a stairway in an abandoned factory and recorded angle grinders cutting steel which are all intergrated on the recordings. Jorgen Sangsta played lead guitars and keyboards. Norwegian photographer Per Talleraas had joined the group in 1986 bringing his film and slide projections to live performances. His photo's were always used on IMH covers and art. Most of the most memorable live performances was during UR Festival at Hennie Onstad Senter near Oslo.

Through being signed to Dossier Records in Berlin. Steve toured for 2 weeks in the DDR (East Germany) in 1988 with Dietmar Diesner. Steve later performed solo at Druga Godba Festval in Slovenia. Steve was also was in the original line up of the Danish chamber group Atlantis Transit who became successful in Denmark with their debut LP 'Tabor' on Olufsen records and a live broadcast on National Danish TV

In 1996 Steve was invited to tour in South Korea as part of Lim Dong Chang's 'World is One' ensemble together Welsh bassist Tony Curly Brooks and Danish saxophonist Henrik Jespersen. 'That was an incredible experience. I learnt a great deal about movement and breathing and space in music through Lim Dong Chang.

In 1996 together with Danish artist Harald Viuff co founded The Hydronorts group in Denmark for very large scale performances. Steve created a series of floating sculptures along with Paul Burwell from Bow Gamelan Ensemble. The sculptures were moored in Kolding Fjord for the Summer of 1996. Later that year The Hydronorts gave large scale performances in Copenhagen harbour which included The Hot pipe Organ – Bastiaan Maris, Geo Homsey and Stock and high voltage sculptor Barry Schwartz.

In 2000 An invitation to participate in The Kortrijk Percussion project led by Belgian master drummer Dirk Wachtelaer and which featured English drummer Trevor Taylor. Dirk was working with his electronic sounds. Trevor Taylor was playing Sculptures Sonores by the Baschet Brothers and Steve was performing on his sound sculptures and percussion creations.

In 2002 In Iceland was founding member of the Icelandic group Jord Bifast together with Egill Johannsson and Siggi Hrellir. Due to logistics Jord Bifast only performed live in Iceland. That same year Steve formed Recreator together with Nick Le Beat and Theo Travis (Soft Machine and Steve Wilson of Porcupine Tree).

Since 1999 Duo performances and recordings with Dutch pioneer sax and reeds improviser Ad Peijnenburg. Also in 1999 Steve began performing and recording with Norwegian saxophonist and clarinetist Frode Gjerstad.

In 2008 Steve was invited to perform on The Large Hot Pipe Organ at Robodock in Amsterdam and Blast in Birmingham. 'I was playing electric drum pads to trigger the explosions in the pipes which was strange as the sound was generated a few seconds later. Recorded in London together with Paul Clarvis on sound sculptures and gongs for the soundtrack to State of Play (Russel Crowe, Ben Aflack and Helen Mirren) The music was composed by Alex Heffes.

In 2009 Steve began performing with the highly respected Celtic harpist Nadia Birkenstock. Their first performance was at the International Harp festival in Selstad outside Barcelona. They have continued since then as The Glow Within. Performing in Germany. Czech Republic. Italy. Netherlands. France. Spain and Portugal.

'I grew up listening to all kinds of music. The first impressions music had on me was hearing the Beatles on the radio when I was 6 years old. When I was 14 Deep Purple made Fireball which had a massive impact on me and I still regard as one of the best rock albums ever and I still listen to it. Influences and inspirations are so many. Here are a few: Deep Purple. Gentle Giant. Chicago – Danny Seraphine and Terry Kath. The Beatles. Black Sabath. Good Habit. Frank Zappa. Andrea Centazzo. Alan Stivell. The Chieftains. Man. Buddy Rich. John Coltrane. Christian Vander. Greenslade – Andy McCulloch. Tony Oxley. Jon Christensen. Daniel Humair. Milford Graves. Alan Holdsworth. Paolo Vinaccia. Terje Rypdal. Hawkwind. Iron Maiden. Samul Nori. Kim Dae Hwan. Lim Dong Chang. Tibetan Ritual music. Einstürzende Neubauten. Iannis Xenakis. Karlheinz Stockhausen. Edgard Varèse. Gert Mortensen. Les Percussions de Strasbourg. JS Bach. Alessandro Scarlatti. Antonio Vivaldi. Antonio Lotti and many more'

Performed/recorded with:

It's My Head. R L Lunding. Splat. Marie Kawatzu. Bob Vatel, Dietmar Diesner. Per Talleraas. Atlantis Transit. Frode Gjerstad, Andrea Centazzo, Loredana Celi. Luca Luciano. Raffaele Barbato. Birgit Lokke, Tineke Noordhoek, David Moss, Paal Nielsen Love, Z'ev. Large Hot Pipe Organ – Bastiaan Marris. Geo Homsey. Stock. Jeffrey Funt. Chico Mac Murtrie. Barry Schwartz. Paul Burwell. Alan Wilkinson. Tony Orrell. Ad Peijnenburg. Dirk Wachtelaer. Vanishing Pictures. Tin Josefsdotter. P O Jorgens. Cyrille Oswald. Tomas Braun. Rodrigo Reijers. George Cremanschi. Antez. Frank Castro and Gumdrum. Joao Pais Filipe. Rui Leal. Filipe Texeira. Henrique Fernandes. Paulo Mesquita. Cortez Lamont III. Robert Glassburner. Gustavo Costa. Alberto Lopez. Carlo Garof, Antonio Bertoni, Stephan Pastor, Geert Tiersma, Peter Brotzmann, Duo with Paulo Mesquita, jörð Bifast with Icelanders Egill Johannsson on guitars and Siggi Hrellir on electronics and atmospherics, Theo Travis and Nick Le'Beat in Recreator and with Theo Travis and Dave Sturt in Cipher, Geuan -Celtic music from Belgium. In 2010 began performing with the great Celtic Harpist Nadia Birkenstock as The Glow Within. Since 2011 performed together with the English sax player George Haslam in various groups and with the Prague based group Freetime who have evolved into something quite unique. Freetime are George Haslam: Tarogato and Baritone sax. Steve Hubback: Percussion. Aida Mujačič: piano and voice. Jozef Láska: Contrabass and Bass guitar. Surrealist, Sorcier, Sonores with Portuguese guitarist Cortez Lamont III

Some of the musicians who perform on Steve's creations include:

Paolo Vinaccia. Michala Østergaard-Nielsen. Tineke Noordhoek. Knut Finsrud. Dame Evelyn Glennie. Carl Palmer. Birgit Lokke, Paul Clarvis, Marilyn Mazure. Paal Nielsen Love. Chris Whitten. Snorre Bjerck. Andrea Centazzo. Peter Fairclough. Alessio Riccio. Thomas Eiler. Welsh National Opera. Gerhard Keimer. Trevor Taylor. Tony Orrell. Gino Robair. Ondrej Smeykal. Carlo Garof. Giorgio Borghini. Davide Merlino. Antonio Bertoni. Jorge Soto Flores. Yuri Pavlovski and Troitsa. Andor Gabor. Job Verweijen and Bill Smith.

Publications:

Fire and Steel: Book about Steve's music and metal creations. Soundworld Publishing England

Featured in Percussion Profiles. Book featuring innovative percussionists. Soundworld Publishing England

Gongs and Tam-Tams: A Guide for Percussionists, Drummers, and Sound Healers by Philip McNamara

Sound Healing with Gongs by Sheila Whittaker

IMPERIAL CYMBALS
Turkey
https://www.instagram.com/imperialcymbals/

IMPRESSION CYMBALS
Turkey
www.impressioncymbals.com

From Website June 2023: Making Cymbals

We take pride in producing our cymbals to meet the highest acoustical and aesthetic standards. Our manufacturing process is not a secret, even though we have learned a trick or two to better the centuries old trade and enhance the end result's grade. It is simply a thoroughly manual craft implemented by master artisans.

In essence, cymbal profile, weight, and the molecular structure of the bronze alloy are the three most important factors for the cymbal characteristics, and this trio forms the basis of our quality.

Casting

As we are making instruments that produce sound by vibrating, the target of the casting process is to make the copper and tin mixture to behave as close to the elements' ideal mechanical properties as possible.

We melt our special B20 formula in max. 50kg pots with very precise measurements using coal fire. This way, the cast bronze that goes into our slow burning wood oven obtains carbon for much-needed elasticity. The molten metal is then poured to molds in order to produce basic cymbals blanks in various sizes.

The cast blanks are repeatedly run through our rolling machine and re-heated. This process is repeated until the aimed size and thickness is reached. At that point the the cymbals are shocked in a pool of water at the highest temperature possible. Even though shocking a cymbal at a high temperature causes it to be very out of shape, we have learned over time that this is the best way to achieve the most successful end result and best quality bronze. However, this also makes the hammering process more difficult and time-consuming. In our industry it is very common to shock the cymbal blanks at low temperatures in order to speed up the manufacturing process and make them suitable for press machines, despite its tendency to drastically lower the cymbal material's acoustic quality.

Casting Bronze
Rolling Blanks
Weighed Blanks
Shocking
Hammering

All our cymbals are hammered and all hammering is done by hand, with different profiles (bow, edges) applied to each size and cymbal model. We hammer and test the cymbals over and over before sending the cymbals for lathing. If the cymbal is not a lathed model, it is simply finished after the last heating and hammering process. In some cases, lathed cymbals are hammered and/or heated again in repeated cycles.

Considering the bell, its size and the pressure it is applying to the center of the cymbal, we can easily say that it plays a big role in the final sound of the cymbal. In accordance with the profile and weight of the cymbal, the bell is heavily influencing its sound character and sustain. In light of this information, we work with a variety of 34 different bell sizes and profiles in order to be prepared to find the exact combination that produces the sound we are after.

ISTANBUL AGOP CYMBALS
Turkey

https://istanbulcymbals.com/
Akcaburgaz Mah. 3038. Sokak No:12 Esenyurt / Istanbul
Phone: + 90 212 886 33 03   Fax: + 90 212 886 33 06
Agop Cymbals Corp. America 3401 Eagle Rock Blvd, Los Angeles, CA 90065
Phone: 213-622-1670   Fax: 213-622-2959
https://istanbulcymbals.com/   info@istanbulcymbals.com   info@istanbulcymbalsusa.com

From the company website:

Our founder, Agop Tomurcuk, was born in Istanbul-Turkey in 1941. Growing up in the Samatya neighborhood of Istanbul, he followed in the footsteps of his older brothers Oksant and Garbis, by beginning work as an apprentice cymbal-smith at the age of 9 at the only cymbal factory in Turkey. Here, Agop learned, and later helped to refine every aspect of the cymbal making process, becoming a master at every process and eventually becoming the chief cymbal-smith, until that company ceased production of their cymbals in Turkey in 1977.

Feeling "like a fish out of water," after a little over a year spent working various odd jobs, Agop became to determined to continue the Turkish tradition of handmade cymbals on his own. With a little bit of asking around, he was able to locate and buy up much of the equipment and tools he used at his previous company. He rented a small workshop in the Bakırköy-Kartaltepe area of Istanbul, and began to experiment and produce some cymbals with the help of his dear wife, Uskui Tomurcuk. But the limited resources and manpower made things very difficult. "At the end of the day, my father's cousin once brought him home by carrying him on his back" explains Agop's son and now company Co-President, Arman Tomurcuk. Eventually, he was able to set up a small, but functional factory and his older brother, Oksant joined the company as chief cymbalsmith. They began by selling cymbals locally to some music stores in Istanbul's Tünel area, but the prospects of this were limited.

Ingiliz Kirkor (left) and Agop Tomurcuk, 1958

Agop Tomurcuk's friend Mehmet Tamdeğer learned of this new venture and offered to become partners. In 1980 they established Zilciler Kollektif Şti. (in English: Cymbal maker Collective), initially using a stenciled, painted Zilciler logo on the cymbals. Over the next two years, Zilciler began to grow and export cymbals internationally. The brand name was soon changed to Istanbul, and by 1982, the company was exporting cymbals to the United States. That same year, Istanbul Cymbals made their debut at the NAMM Show in The United States, where legendary drummer Mel Lewis declared "They're Back!" referring to the sound of his beloved hand-hammered vintage Turkish cymbals. Mel became our first endorser and our association with him has been a great honor for us ever since. In 1984, Agop's eldest son, and now company Co-President, Sarkis Tomurcuk, officially joined the company. There was a growing demand for the cymbals, and it was difficult to even fill orders. "At the time, we were 9 or 10 persons working in the workshop and my father was very disciplined. My father always forced Arman and I to work much more than anybody else, so that we could understand every single detail about the art of cymbal making. The production process, in those days was much more difficult. "We used to work with charcoal heaters to melt the alloy for casting. After melting, I had to carry a 55-60 kg bronze filled melting pot between my legs with a special lifting device that we had fabricated, and then pour the melted alloy into pans very carefully so that it wouldn't splash. The temperature inside the melting pot would often exceed 1000 C, so I would first soak my pants with cold water, in order to avoid burning myself. My pants would become dry from the heat before I even began to pour the alloy into pans. The whole thing would take maybe 7 or 8 seconds and my pants would begin to burn if I took too long. This is how we cast every single cymbal at the time. When I think about it now I can't believe how we managed" says Sarkis.

In 1986 Agop's younger son, and now company Co-President Arman Tomurcuk officially joined the company. From 1986 until 1996, Istanbul Cymbals continued to grow considerably, and gain the recognition and admiration of many of the greatest musicians, many of whom visited the factory from all parts of the world. "When I was 14, my father took me see Elvin Jones perform in Istanbul. It was a great concert. Afterwards, we went backstage. I was wearing an Istanbul t-shirt. Elvin saw me and he came right over to me with this huge smile and autographed my t-shirt. I still keep that precious present from Elvin. The next day, he visited our workshop. It was one of the greatest moments of my life" explains Arman. During this era, Billy Hart, Tony Williams, Danny Gottlieb, Jack Dejohnette, Art Blakey, Cindy Blackman and many others came to visit. In 1992, Arman completed his education in England and returned to Istanbul. In 1993, he attended the Musikmesse trade show, and helped to expand the company's distribution to 30 countries worldwide.

After Oksant's retirement, Sarkis became the chief cymbalsmith in the company. After a tragic accident, company founder Agop Tomurcuk passed away in 1996. After their father's death, the two brothers quit the old factory where they had worked for 16 years and formed Istanbul Zilciler in 1997, further distinguishing themselves with the Istanbul Agop brand name and adopting a more progressive approach toward sounds and designs, while staying true to the tradition. By 1998, the Alchemy Series was created to expand our sound beyond traditional Jazz cymbals and better suit a diverse range of more modern and higher volume music.

In 2004, Istanbul Agop opened the first company owned office outside of Istanbul, in Los Angeles, California, USA to further improve our relationship with artists and drummers, and further expand the availability of our instruments. In 2005, we released our 25th Anniversary Ride as an expression of our continuing journey to push the limits of traditional cymbal making, while staying true to the ancient tradition. In 2022, we have the most musical and diverse and innovative cymbal lineup anywhere, supported by a roster of the most influential and compelling drummers of this generation.

This is where the journey of B20 Bronze starts. Basically B20 Bronze alloy is a mixture of 80% Copper and 20% Tin and B20 is known as the most musical of all alloys. The highest quality raw materials are used to produce our B20 alloy.

Our centuries old secret process gives the alloy its strength, durability and flexibility. Without the secret process, the metal will be hard but very brittle and can break like a glass easily.

That secret process has an extremely important role on producing musical sounding cymbals.

In the very first step of producing cast cymbals, the proper mixture of metals are melted and combined in the melting pot which they soon become castings. Melting allows the copper and tin mix in a certain heat and that heat evaporates all impurities in the alloy. Now the molten alloy is ready to be poured into molds to become castings.

The molten alloy in the melting pot is directly poured in to the molds. The amount of the molten alloy in every mold can be different depending on the cymbal type. After pouring, the alloy gets hardened and becomes what we call Castings. Castings are removed from the molds with extreme care and grouped according to their weights. Now these castings are ready for the next step which we call "Heating"..

The castings are now ready to be heated around 700-800 C in our oven. Each casting is heated evenly in the oven by our skilled craftsmen. The heated castings are now soft and ready to go under the rolling machine to become metal discs which we call "blanks". These blanks are heated up and rolled again several times until the blank reaches its desired thickness. This process also allows the metal molecules bond together perfectly and makes the metal more durable. Then blanks are set aside to cool before the next process.

Cooled down blanks are now ready for bell pressing but at this phase, the blanks are still very brittle and oversized. After marking the center of the blanks for the bell, they are send to oven one more time in order to make the metal soft and pliable again for pressing. The bell is pressed into the hot blank and a little guide hole is punched into the center of the bell. Finally, blanks are tempered and getting ready for annealing process which is one of the most important parts of cymbal making. Red hot blanks are placed into cool water and this hot-cold process takes the strength of metal to a new level. Now the B20 is more durable, flexible and musical then ever. After cutting the blanks into their proper shape, all the excess metal is send to be recycled. Now the properly shaped blanks are ready for the next step.

This process is the first and the most important phase of shaping the sound of a cymbal. Hammering is done by our skilled craftsmen, using centuries old hammering techniques. These techniques determine the dark, complex and musical sound qualities of Traditional Turkish Cymbals. In its nature, hammering process requires mastery, skill and lots of hard work cause in handmade cymbals, the profile of a cymbal is given only by hammer hits. For example an 16" Crash has got approximately 1500 hammer hits. The profile of each blank is different from each other which means the amount of hammer hits required, can differ from cymbal to cymbal. This results in different sounding cymbals even in the same series, same sizes. That makes every cymbal sound unique and makes every player who uses our cymbals sound unique.

Lathing is the other very important phase of cymbal making which directly effects the sound of a cymbal. It should definitely be done by highly skilled craftsmen. Lathing cuts circular grooves on a cymbal and lets the vibrations travel on the surface of a cymbal easily. Also lathing helps to cut down the cymbal to its proper thickness. Depending on the series, some cymbals are lathed both on top and bottom, some only on top or on the bottom and some without any lathing. The cymbals which are unlathed, remain darker, dryer and dirtier in sound. Comparing to the unlathed cymbals, lathed cymbals are more open sounding, respond quicker and has got more sustain. Several types of blades, shaving techniques and pressure are used to get different sounds out of B20 Alloy. After the lathing, the rough edges and the center holes are smoothed out by a craftsman and cymbals are ready for the final process.

ISTANBUL MEHMET

https://www.istanbulmehmet.com/

Istanbul Mehmet Headquarters / Factory
SANAYI MAHALLESI
(EVREN OTO SANAYI SITESI) 1691 SOKAK
NO.5-7-9, HOŞDERE YOLU
34510
ESENYURT- ISTANBUL / TURKEY
TELEPHONE: 90 212 672 16 01 - 672 65 22
info@istanbulmehmet.com

ISTANBUL MEHMET CYMBALS USA
68-805 PEREZ ROAD F-26
CATHEDRAL CITY, CA, 92234
TELEPHONE: +1 818 641 3087
usasales@istanbulmehmet.com

Website history:

Mehmet Tamdeger learned his art from Mikhail Zilcan, the grandson of Kerope Zilcan, after whom the Zilcan K series is named. In the 1950s, he worked in the K. Zilcan factory in Istanbul. At the age of nine Mehmet Tamdeger started to work for Mikhail Zilcan. Mikhail Zilcan and Kirkor Kucukyan taught him every aspect of this ancient Turkish art, based on a history that stems back to the early 17th century. The Istanbul brand name was adopted by a cymbal works established by two cymbal smiths, Mehmet Tamdeger and Agop Tomurcuk. At that time, they had over three decades of cymbal making experience. Mehmet and Agop named their company after the city that has been home to the epitome of high quality cymbals for many, many years: Istanbul. These cymbals were first exported to the U.S. in 1984, first under the name "Zildjiler", and soon afterwards as "Istanbul". Both craftsmen signed each cymbal and many of these cymbals are now collectors' items. After Agop Tomurcuk's unexpected death in July 1996, Mehmet decided to continue the production of cymbals under his own name, İstanbul Mehmet. A lot has changed since then, but his belief in the richness and the character of a handmade cymbal will always remain. Machines don't have ears. That's why we continue to make our cymbals according to the ancient tradition - with an open eye towards the music that's being made now, and in the future.

ISTANBUL PERA
Turkey

Galipdede Cad. No:2/E Tunel / Beyoglu   ISTANBUL   +90 (212) 244 5761
http://istanbulperacymbals.com   info@istanbulpera.com

We never give up of;
Traditional ground fire places (only made from baked clay),
Stone stove ovens (special pavement base),
Wood and charcoal,
Sacred elements air, water, fire and earth,
We combined and used them wherever and whenever necessary, as needed.

JOHAN NICOLAS JANICKE
France

https://www.facebook.com/cymbalartisan
https://www.youtube.com/channel/UCxASfrwupgUjILqwNv9N3aw
jnjanicke@gmail.com

KL CUSTOM CYMBALS
Croatia

Kruno Levacic   https://www.facebook.com/kruno.levacic
https://vimeo.com/user13006000

KMCIC CYMBALS
Poland
https://www.facebook.com/kmiciccymbals
https://kmiciccymbals.com/ office@kmiciccymbals.com

KAMIN CYMBALS
Germany
https://www.instagram.com/kamincymbals/
https://www.facebook.com/KaminCymbals/

KASZA Cymbals
Office in USA, Manufacturing in Wuhan, China
https://bigbangdist.com/brands/kasza-cymbals/

OLIVER KERN CYMBALS
Germany
https://www.oliverkerncymbals.de/ oliverkern@gmx.net
Call me: 0761 29 232 83 0177 28 523 63
Oliver Kern Cymbals Karlstrasse 69 79104 Freiburg im Breisgau

Handmade cymbals from cymbalsmith located in germany. I order my blanks directly from one of the big turkish foundries in Istanbul. These get hand hammered and lathed in my little workshop in Freiburg, germany. You can play them in my workshop.

GREGG KEPLINGER
USA
https://www.keplingerdrums.com/ greggkeplinger@gmail.com

Gregg Keplinger is a rare hybrid of drumming talent and percussive artisan. Early in his career, Gregg toured Mexico straight out of high school, worked with the house band for a circus, haunted the halls of his jazz-drumming hero Elvin Jones in New York, and worked closely in-studio and on stage with a young Matt Cameron during Soundgarden's "Superunknown" glory days and continued on with Matt to work with Pearl Jam.

After finding a 1930s Ludwig 6.5x14" steel snare with an otherworldly tone and a price to match, Gregg followed in the footsteps of the elite class of drum craftsmen to which he now belongs - he improvised and innovated. Sourcing stainless steel from an industrial pipe manufacturer in Seattle, Gregg set to building the first of many custom snare drums, and thus the "Keplinger" vision - for hefty metal-shell snares, and percussion with an industrial personality - was born. Fittingly, Elvin Jones was the proud recipient of one of "Kep's" first snare drums.

KOIDE CYMBALS
Japan
http://koidecymbal.com/factory/index.html

Koide Production

In 1947, Toshio Koide's father and two brothers opened a metal processing facility. For a brief period during the 1960's, they produced entry-level cymbals and later began fabricating kettles for orchestral timpani, which they continued for 23 years. In 1998, Toshio decided to return to cymbal-making, using readily available B8 bronze. Toshio started Koide Cymbals' first production made cymbal line in 2003. Shortly thereafter, he began utilizing Turkish made B20 blanks and traditional cymbal-making practices. As he developed his understanding of standard cymbal fabrication and the qualities of the B20 alloy, he decided to expand on his understanding of cymbal metallurgy and the physics of cymbal sound characteristics. Toshio found guidance from such noted facilities as Research Institute for Applied Sciences, Industrial Technology Center of Fukui Perfecture, University of Fukui, and Osaka Alloying Works Company Ltd. This extensive research led to new alloys and production techniques – and new cymbal sounds.

Koide Cymbals are distinctive, the results of primarily B23ZT and B21ZFe, which are Koide's patented alloys of Zirconium, Titanium, Iron, and higher Tin to Copper ratios. Each cymbal series is manufactured by methods specific to that series, so each series has unique and distinctly different qualities. Koide still uses his own B20 alloy and traditional hammering methods for his more Turkish sounding 703 cymbal line as well. All of Koide's cymbal blank material is specially produced in Japan for Koide Cymbal Co. by a foundry that specializes in copper-based alloys using highly sophisticated processing techniques to manufacture his proprietary alloys.

Comments from Burke Daugerty, June 2024:

Toshi's approach was one of reverse engineering cymbal mechanics through scientific study with a university physics department, then exploring metallurgy and manufacturing practices to create new cymbal sounds. He is not a musician, an interesting point on its own, but has a sincere passion for cymbals as instruments and in metallurgy. This is not as a means for commercial gain as one might mistakenly take away from his approach and tropes about Japanese production. His is a more modern take on traditional japanese craftsmanship and cultural exploration. He is currently participating in a funded study on the connection between the psychological and sensory perception vs the actual physical/acoustic properties of what makes a cymbal "Dark", why we throw that term around so much in describing a cymbal's sonic characteristics, and its loose interpretation and relevancy in topical discussion. Cool stuff!

Burke Daugherty interview with Toshio Koide

BD: Please give a brief history of your background such as: early life, education/study, work history, and connection to music/cymbals

TK: After I graduated from college, I started working at my father's sheet metal processing company. I had connection with cymbals when "Koide Works" used to make brass cymbals in 1960s and timpani kettle from 1979 to 2002.

BD: How did you come to begin making cymbals, what was it that inspired you to begin making cymbals?

TK: I started research on cymbals when we had an employee who played drums for his hobby. He told us there is no cymbal maker in Japan and suggested that we begin.

BD: When did you start making cymbals in your own way?

TK: I started research on cymbals in 1997 and we started selling B8 cymbals in 2003.

BD: Was there any particular person(s) that influenced you?

TK: I was influenced by Zildjan company's modern manufacturing methods.

BD: What was the factor that made you interested in developing your alloys and manufacturing approach? Did you do your own analysis of Turkish bronze alloys? If so, did you discover a difference between older and modern alloys in Turkish cymbal bronze?

TK: We started making cymbals from B20 cymbal alloys imported from Turkey, but we faced many problems. That led us to research making own alloys but we didn't know how to make the bronze casting. Fortunately, we found Osaka Alloy Works.,Co to take over that part and make our unique alloys for making cymbals. We first analyzed the material makeup of the Zildjan cymbal, the Turkish cymbal, the Paiste cymbal and the Chinese cymbal. From this analysis and beyond, we did research on the differences in metallic properties depending on microstructure of metals because Osaka Alloy Works produces superconducting materials that are very similar to cymbal alloys.

BD: How did you begin to work with the Physics Department, and what was perhaps your biggest discovery?

TK: Our research of metallic properties was led by finding the different characteristics between Paiste's B8 and B15 cymbals, Zildjan's B20 cymbal, and the Turkish B20 cymbal. We started by studying the reasons for these differences.

BD: How did you apply the research to your current methods of cymbal production?

TK: We learned that cymbal vibrations will change when different tin content and additives are used. Because of this, we made the new B23 cymbal material, which is different from traditional cymbal material by having more tin content for more durability. However, this material was very difficult to shape it into a cymbal, so we thought adding different additives, such as titanium, zirconium, and iron may make this possible. As a result, now we have 4 types of cymbal materials to manufacture cymbals.

BD: Did you work with any Turkish masters while developing your alloys?

TK: I imported 2 to 3 different Turkish company's cymbal materials, but never worked with them before. I also developed my own way of manufacturing cymbals.

BD: Have there been any studies comparing traditional Turkish alloys and the alloys you developed with Osaka Metal Works? Is there such a thing as a typical Turkish B20 alloy? Do you feel the differences in older vs newer cymbals are more from the aging process or the alloy itself?

TK: From our research, we know that the traditional method of casting cymbal material and Osaka Alloy Works' method of casting cymbal material are completely different. Because of the different casting methods, the metal structures are different and cymbal sounds are different. We manufacture our cymbals using Osaka Alloy Works' B20 cymbal material, so the sound of the cymbal is little bit different than Turkish cymbals.

BD: As you researched the connections between scientific analysis of bronze and the sonic results, was that research driven by any particular goals such as producing particular tones that are desired by players?

TK: My first goal of manufacturing the cymbal was to improve durability of cymbals and that led us to research on new cymbal materials.

BD: Did the research lead to new methods of production?

TK: I know we are different from the way of Turkish cymbals are manufactured, but I am not sure how Zildjan makes cymbals, so it may be similar. However, we make 703 Series cymbals using only hammers, which is same as Turkish cymbals.

BD: Can you give a brief overview of the alloy research and how it guided your cymbal development. What was it you felt was missing in a typical B20 in terms of sound or manufacturing for the methods you currently use?

TK: As I said, we began our research by increasing the durability of cymbals. After some research, we were able to produce a material that stopped cymbal vibrations quickly by adding zirconium and iron. For example, B23 titanium material transmits vibrations quickly, but B21 zirconium and iron material has slower and shorter transmission of vibration. These differences make our Koide cymbals' series easy to understand and also give unique characteristics to each. I believe it is very difficult to characterize cymbals by weight, size and hammering like traditional cymbal making.

BD: What new areas of research are you working on currently or researching in the future?

TK: The cymbal materials are very hard and difficult to mold, so the pitch becomes different. We are currently developing the manufacturing method to control pitches of the cymbals.

BD: Is there anything else you'd like to add to this interview that has been overlooked that we should know about you or your cymbals? Please feel free to share anything you'd like here.

TK: At our company, Koide cymbal, we are currently manufacturing 6 series of cymbals using 4 different materials:

Brilliant Series (B23 titanium),
Eolian Series (B22 iron),
Absolute Series (B21 zirconium/iron),
Cadence Series (B20 titanium),
703 Series (B20 titanium)
10J Series (B20 titanium).

It my pleasure to know many people will experience the difference of these cymbals!

Toshio KOIDE's research while affiliated with The Japan Steel Works, Ltd and other places

While most cymbal smiths learn primarily through trial & error, Toshio Koide has engaged in a great deal of scientific research. Some of the papers he has authored or co-authored are listed her and can be accessed online through ResearchGate.Net through the link below.

https://www.researchgate.net/scientific-contributions/Toshio-KOIDE-2117094100

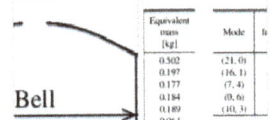

Effect of bell size on sound characteristics of cymbalsシンバルの音響特性に及ぼすベルサイズの影響

December 2019

Transactions of the JSME (in Japanese)

Wataru OGAWA · Fumiyasu Kuratani · Tatsuya YOSHIDA · [...] · Taiji MIZUTA

Cymbals are percussion instruments that vibrate and radiate sounds when hit with a stick. A bell is the raised section in the middle of the cymbal and its size produces different sounds. In this study, we investigate the effect of bell size on the sound characteristics of cymbals. The radiated sounds and vibrations for cymbals with two different bell sizes are measured. In addition, the natural frequency and mode shape are obtained by finite element analysis and the sound radiation efficiency is calculated for each mode. The measured results indicate that the sound frequency characteristics for the large bell show three peaks with large sound pressure within the range of 1000 to 3000 Hz and the sound pressure for the small bell is larger than that for the large bell within the range of 4000 to 5000 Hz. The vibration frequency characteristics show there is no remarkable difference between the large and small bells. The sound radiation efficiencies indicate that the large bell has many modes with high radiation efficiency within the range of 1000 to 3000 Hz and their modes have a small number of nodal diameters and a large deformation at the bell. The small bell has many modes with high efficiency within the range of 4000 to 5000 Hz. This is reason for the difference in sound characteristics between the large and small bells.

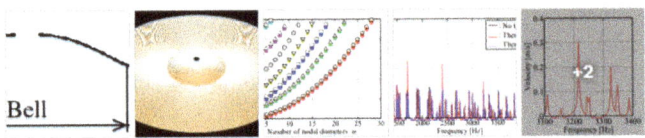

Understanding the effect of hammering process on the vibration characteristics of cymbals

September 2016

Journal of Physics Conference Series

Fumiyasu Kuratani · T Yoshida · T Koide · [...] · Kozo Osamura

Cymbals are thin domed plates used as percussion instruments. When cymbals are struck, they vibrate and radiate sound. Cymbals are made through spin forming, hammering, and lathing. The spin forming creates the basic shape of the cymbal, which determines its basic vibration characteristics. The hammering and lathing produce specific sound adjustments by changing the cymbal's vibration characteristics. In this study, we study how hammering cymbals affects their vibration characteristics. The hammering produces plastic deformation (small, shallow dents) on the cymbal's surface, generating residual stresses throughout it. These residual stresses change the vibration characteristics. We perform finite element analysis of a cymbal to obtain its stress distribution and the resulting change in vibration characteristics. To reproduce the stress distribution, we use thermal stress analysis, and then with this stress distribution we perform vibration analysis. These results show that each of the cymbal's modes has a different sensitivity to the thermal load (i.e., hammering). This difference causes changes in the frequency response and the deflection shape that significantly improves the sound radiation efficiency. In addition, we explain the changes in natural frequencies by the stress and modal strain energy distributions.

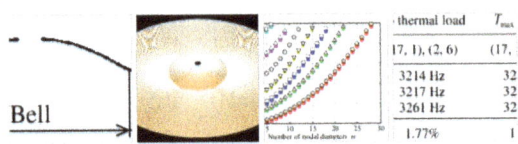

Effect of Metal Structure on Damping Characteristics of Cymbals

February 2019

Journal of the Japan Institute of Metals and Materials

Wataru Ogawa · Takahisa Shobu · Mizue Kakehi · [...] · Taiji Mizuta

Cymbals are percussion musical instruments with a simpler structure than other musical instruments. Therefore, their material composition basically decides the sound quality and decay time rather than the skill of the player. In this study, specimens of cymbals to which Titanium, Zirconium and Iron were added were prepared. From the difference of diffraction rings by synchrotron radiation X-rays, the crystal structure of the specimens of cymbals prepared by various manufacturing processes was analyzed in order to investigate the relationship between the crystal structure associated with the material and manufacturing process used and the damping of the sound of cymbals. As a result, it was found that the changes in the crystal structure were due to the manufacturing process used. In addition, it was clarified that the changes affected the damping of the sound of cymbals. Fig. 10 Diffraction pattern of 21F, 21ZF and 23ZT after spinning. Fullsize Image

Toshio KOIDE's research while affiliated with The Japan Steel Works, Ltd and other places

How the hammering process of cymbals affects their vibration characteristics

July 2017

Transactions of the JSME (in Japanese)

Fumiyasu Kuratani · Kento KITABAYASHI · Wataru OGAWA · [...] · Taiji MIZUTA

Cymbals are percussion instruments that vibrate and radiate sounds when hit with a stick or when used in pairs. The sound radiated from a cymbal depends on its vibration characteristics. Cymbals are made through spin forming, hammering and lathing processes. The spin forming creates the domed shape of cymbals, determining the basic vibration characteristics. The hammering and lathing make specific sound quality adjustments by changing the vibration characteristics. In this paper, we focus on how the hammering affects the cymbal's vibration characteristics. The hammering produces many shallow dents over the cymbal's surface, generating residual stresses in it. These residual stresses change the vibration characteristics. We perform finite element analysis of the hammered cymbal to obtain its vibration characteristics. In the analysis, we use thermal stress analysis to reproduce the stress distribution and then with this stress distribution we perform vibration analysis. The results show that the effects of thermal load (i.e., hammering) vary depending on the mode: an increase or decrease in the natural frequency. As a result, the peak frequencies and their peak values in the frequency response function change.

The Correlation Between the Percussive Sound and the Residual Stress/Strain Distributions in a Cymbal

October 2016

Journal of Materials Engineering and Performance

Kozo Osamura · Fumiyasu Kuratani · Toshio Koide · [...] · Takahisa Shobu

The artistic sound of a cymbal is produced by employing a special copper alloy as well as incorporating complicated and heterogeneous residual stress/strain distributions. In order to establish a modern engineering process that achieves high-quality control for the cymbals, it is necessary to investigate the distribution of the residual stresses/strains in the cymbal and their quantitative relation with the frequency characteristics of the sound generated from the cymbal. In the present study, we have successfully used synchrotron radiation to measure the distribution of residual strain in two kinds of cymbals—after spinforming as well as after hammering. The microstructure and the mechanical properties of the cymbals were measured as well their acoustic response. Based on our experimental data, the inhomogeneous residual stress/strain distributions in the cymbals were deduced in detail and their influence on the frequency characteristics of the sound produced by the cymbals was identified.

Understanding the effect of hammering process on the vibration characteristics of cymbals

September 2016

Journal of Physics Conference Series

Fumiyasu Kuratani · T Yoshida · T Koide · [...] · Kozo Osamura

How the sound adjustment process of cymbals affects their vibration and sound radiation characteristics

October 2016

The Journal of the Acoustical Society of America

Fumiyasu Kuratani · Tatsuya Yoshida · Toshio Koide · [...] · Kozo Osamura

Cymbals are percussion instruments. They vibrate and radiate sounds when hit with a drumstick or when used in pairs and the sounds depend on the vibration characteristics. Cymbals are made through spin forming, hammering and lathing. The spin forming creates the domed shape of the cymbal, determining its basic vibration characteristics. The hammering and lathing produce specific sound adjustments by changing the vibration characteristics. In this study, we focus on how the hammering affects the vibration and sound radiation characteristics. The hammering produces many shallow dents over the cymbal's surface, generating residual stresses in it. These residual stresses change the vibration characteristics. We perform finite element analysis of the hammered cymbal to obtain its vibration and sound radiation characteristics. In the analysis, we use thermal stress analysis to reproduce the stress distribution and then with this stress distribution we perform vibration analysis. The results show that the effect of thermal load (i.e., hammering) depends on mode: an increase or decrease in the natural frequency. The difference between the modes changes the peak frequencies and their amplitudes in the frequency response. As a result, the deflection shapes and their sound radiation efficiencies at the peak frequencies are changed.

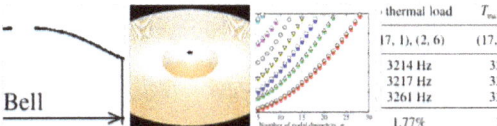

Effect of sound adjustment processing on the vibration behavior of cymbals

January 2016

The Proceedings of the Dynamics & Design Conference

Kento KITABAYASHI · Tasuku ISHIHARA · Fumiyasu Kuratani · [...] · Kozo Osamura

Cymbals are thin domed plates used as percussion instruments. When cymbals are stuck, they vibrate and radiate sound. Cymbals are made through spin forming, hammering, and lathing. The sound radiated from a cymbal depends on its vibration characteristics that are determined by the shape and dimension. The hammering produces plastic deformation on the cymbal's surface, generating residual stresses throughout it. Although the vibration characteristics are changed by the hammering to adjust cymbal sound, the effect of the hammering on the cymbal sound is not clear. In this paper, we reveal the effect of the hammering on the vibration and the sound radiation characteristics. The stress distribution within the cymbal produced by hammering is reproduced by thermal stress analysis and the change in natural frequency of the modes are calculated by the vibration analysis with the stress distribution. The change (i.e., increase or decrease) in natural frequency for each mode is explained by the stress and modal strain energy distributions.

The Correlation Between the Percussive Sound and the Residual Stress/Strain Distributions in a Cymbal

October 2016

Journal of Materials Engineering and Performance

Kozo Osamura · Fumiyasu Kuratani · Toshio Koide · [...] · Takahisa Shobu

... More than a hundred normal modes were identified using experimental measurements validated by Finite Element Method (FEM) simulations in [6,7]. The correlation between the percussive sound and the residual stress/strain distributions in a cymbal was studied in [8], while the effect of the manufacturing process of hammering on the vibrational behaviour of cymbals was evaluated in [9] via FEM simulations. Nonlinear vibrations of plates with variable thickness and their application to synthesising cymbals sounds were investigated in [10,11]. ...

Reference: *FEM-BEM Vibroacoustic Simulations of Motion Driven Cymbal-Drumstick Interactions*

LEGADO CYMBALS
Turkey
https://www.legadocymbals.com/

established in 2017, "Designed in California, produced in Turkey by master cymbal smiths"

From the website: If you can dream it, we can build it. Our Alchemist series offers complete customization. We craft any cymbal to any specifications, allowing you to create your sonic masterpiece with world-class aesthetics.

DAVID LA MELA
Belgium
https://www.instagram.com/dee_la_mela/   https://www.facebook.com/david.lamela.50

LEON CYMBALS
Turkey
https://www.leoncymbals.com
leon@leoncymbals.com   baran@leoncymbals.com

100 % handmade: we are one of the few remaining representatives of those legendary Turkish cymbal Making tradition. Cymbals that are melted with coal, fired with wood, hammered and lathed by hand. We are one of the few manufacturers who reject all of the changes in cymbal production techniques, which are made in order to utilize more numbers in production and abandoned the classical methods of cymbal making. As Leon Cymbals, we are a cymbal brand that produces only the highest quality of cymbals in limited numbers. We record every product we produce to stand behind our claim. We are a manufacturer that has been making cymbals for 15 years. (Since 2008)

KUPO
Singapore
https://www.youtube.com/@doranoon10   @doranoon1
hiyo im doran i make cymbals & stuff @kupobuilds

STEFAN LEIBINGER
Germany
https://beck-ham.de

LIUS CYMBALS
Sweden
https://www.liuscymbals.com/   @liuscymbals

David Lius produces cymbals made from Turkish blanks.

MADEJSKI Cymbals Mfg
Poland
https://www.fmadejskicymbals.com/

    Cymbals have fascinated me for a long time. In experimental music and sound art that I have dealt with as a drummer and composer, nuances and specific sound qualities played a special role for me. The possibility of deconstructing meanings and ways of using available instruments have constituted the ground for my interest in the design and the method of producing cymbals. My own observations, research about the production of cymbals including technological and material consultations have led me to the point where I have started to build workshop and collect tools for artisan processing of the legendary bronze alloy with 20 percent tin content - an alchemical key to the world of these extraordinary instruments with centuries of tradition and roots dating back to several millennia.

    A significant moment in learning about problems of different stages of the cymbals production was for me the encounter with a small but extremely inspiring world of independent cymbalsmiths - acting somewhat in opposition to highly repetitive high-volume production. Despite the different methods, principles and working in different conditions, independent cymbalsmiths are using creatively achievements, recipes, traditions and experiences of leading producers. Among other things, it is the activity of these artisan outsiders with a variety of technical approaches and creative attitudes, which gave me faith in my own research, ideas and ventures. After stage of reconnaissance and preparations, I have finally set up my workshop in May 2019. The effects of this process as well as the process itself are the subject of this page.

    My bio: Filip Madejski (born in 1987 in Warsaw, Poland) is a musician, audiovisual maker and producer, experimental drummer and composer. From 2010 to 2016 he studied at the Faculty of Media Arts of the Academy of Fine Arts in Warsaw. He took part in numerous music projects at the intersection of discourses and disciplines of art. Since 2019 he has being developing an independent cymbal workshop F. Madejski Cymbals Manufacture. He lives and works in Warsaw.   ©2020 by F. Madejski Cymbals Manufacture Warsaw

MARCUS CYMBALS
Argentina
https://marcuscymbals.com.ar/

I am Marcus Lanzarotti, a native of San Fernando, north of Greater Buenos Aires. My first contact with the instrument was at the age of 13, with an innate passion for metals, I became fascinated by cymbals. One of the reasons why I started studying Mechanical Engineering was the dream of setting up a factory one day, but then the large imports from China, with great price/quality competitiveness, led my thoughts to other directions.

After finishing my engineering degree and stimulated by a great teacher I had, I started an investigation to make professional quality handmade dishes. And motivated by the work of other independent artisans around the world such as Roberto Spicicchino in Italy; Matt Bettis in California; Matt Nolan in England or Craig Lauritsen in Australia, I began to have my own experience in the art of the hammer, shaping the first cymbals in 2014, building my first lathe, researching suitable cutting materials and testing in practice. I started with brass, without consistent acoustic results, until in 2016 I met my teacher in this beautiful profession, Francisco Domene, and I had my first contacts with blanks (raw material in the shape of a round plate,

Since 2019 I only work with B20 bronze from the Domene Cymbals factory in Brazil, since it is an alloy that only cymbal factories produce. During 2019/20 I was working in two places, on the one hand in my workshop in the San Fernando district, Greater Buenos Aires; on the other, I have traveled to the city of Avaré-SP, Brazil to help my teacher Francisco Domene and improve my skills as a craftsman. As of September 2020 I am working as a craftsman for Domene Cymbals in Avaré-SP, Brazil. I visit Buenos Aires 2 or 3 times a year and at those times I take the opportunity to do acoustic modification work on cymbals from other brands. Any questions I pay attention by private message through my Instagram @marcuscymbals

MASTERWORK
Turkey
www.facebook.com/Masterwork-Cymbals-Offi…74351469436399/
https://www.masterwork.com.tr/

B25 alloy , the combination of the copper and tin, the secret formul is being used for mant years for the great musical sound by the musicians all over the world. This alloy is a matter of passion , desire and sadness that the cymbals smith takes out deep his heart and soul.

Masterwork Cymbals factory founded in 2002 in Istanbul and now owned by the cymbal cmith Yucel ULUC and darbouka smith Cetin LIMONCU . The factory manufactures 14 different series on the tradational B25 Alloy. The cymbals leave the factory hand signed after being checked by specialist fort he best quality and get delivered allover the world. This is the main philosophy of our company

MEHTERAN
Turkey

Kirazlık Mah. Örnek Sanayi Sitesi 1033. Cadde No:10 55330 Tekkeköy,
SAMSUN, TURKEY
https://www.mehterancymbals.com/
0090 545 280 6516   0090 544 876 7899
mehterancymbals@gmail.com   info@mehterancymbals.com
https://www.instagram.com/mehterancymbals/
https://www.facebook.com/mehterancymbals/
https://www.youtube.com/channel/UCckDCiTmwFhn0xfXyY_2VTw

My name is Adem DIRIL. First I became a cymbal smith in the turkish part of the company of Meinl in 2006. Since 15 years I have experience in many kind of cymbals. My main reason is to produce 100% hand made cymbals and use only B-20 metal.

In 2021 I decided to build my own brand, MEHTERAN CYMBALS, available with big cymbal range in all over the world. Mehteran cymbals each are hand made with our proven technique and the finest quality materials, all here in our beautiful land of Turkey.

MEINL
Production in Germany and Turkey
https://meinlcymbals.com/

Byzance foundry series, B20 made in Turkey

MIKE MONGIELLO

Mike Mongiello is an Independent Cymbalsmith hailing from Philadelphia, Pennsylvania. He began his journey as a maker after obsessing over his own cymbal sound palette while playing in bands across many styles for over 20 years.

Having no prior experience in metalworking, Mike began creating exclusively in the stainless steel format to teach himself the basics of cold-impact shaping. Before long he graduated himself to work in Turkish b20 bronze, attracting the attention of Master Cymbalsmith Francisco Domene, who extended an invitation to study traditional methods at his factory in Avaré, Brazil.

Now, operating in a small workshop in South Philadelphia, Mike crafts each instrument from start to finish by hand with the finest materials available.

After years of blood, sweat and bronze, having sold hundreds of cymbals to drummers all over the world, Mike Mongiello is proud to be one the few full-time professional Cymbalsmiths currently working in the United States.
Examples of Mike's work can be found on his website, mongiellocymbals.com, or through Instagram at @mongiello_cymbals.

https://mongiellocymbals.com/

https://mongiellocymbals.com/

Mike Mongiello is an independent cymbalsmith from Philadelphia, Pennsylvania. Since February of 2019, he has been hand-hammering cymbals and gongs using handmade and self-modified tools. He began after years of research and tool development, inspired by the work of Dave Collingwood, Nicky Moon, Matt Bettis, Matt Nolan, Philippe Gauthier Boudreau and the late great Roberto Spizzichino among other great makers from around the globe. Although his journey started alone, he has progressed with the support and advice of the international cymbalsmith community. In March of 2020, Mike traveled to Avaré, Brazil to meet his mentor and friend Fransisco Domene. There he studied traditional and modern hammering and lathing techniques to further develop his skills. Now, back home in South Philly, he continues practicing his craft as one of the few professional cymbalsmiths in the world.

Comments excerpted from the Mongiello interview at the 2023 Chicago Drum Show

I got a set of "custom" cymbals from one of the big companies, but they were not really for me. I started hearing about Spizzochino and Matt Bettis and Craig Lauritsen, and Steve Hubbeck- man, that guy! If you want to see some weird stuff- Steve Hubbeck- that guy rules! And Matt Nolan. And all of these people that are now in front of my; Dave Collingwood, Nicky Moon. I was like- ok, you can do that. So how do you do that? The short answer is you get a hammer and anvil and then you're a cymbal smith. The journey is very long to GOOD cymbal smith. It becomes your life very quickly.

I started working in only stainless steel. I got an anvil and chopped up some hammers- I knew at the time that I could get stainless steel a little bit cheaper than bronze and I didn't want to ruin a ton of bronze so I did about a year of all stainless steel. Then I started ordering some bronze and caught some people's attention, including Francisco Domene from Brazil. He invited me to his factory in Brazil and I did some training with him. I've also done some training with Nicky Moon and some work with Dave Collingwood. I don't do the cloning thing, but I was able to visit Eric Binder and study the curvature and bells of about 40 old K's and decide for myself what I liked about them and what I didn't like- I didn't like the ones that were really super tall in terms of profile- the umbrella profile. I did like them when they started to umbrella out then became a little bit flatter. And liked the smaller, shallower bells. I know that a lot of those were in Europe, the shallower bells. It seems like we got a lot of the bigger (taller) bells with the cymbals that were imported by Gretsch. So for the Prestige Series that I made for Eric, I did hand formed bells. They are very flat, wide bells that give a lower tone and the overtones don't get crazy out of control. You get your stick but you get the presence of having a bell.

I love to improvise, to just start out with a piece of metal and let it become what it's going to be; to work on it until it's done. I do have "ranges"- I have a series called WorkHorse, which is a traditional series. It's hammered and fully lathed and meant to be whatever you want it to be.... choose the bell, choose the weight, and it's going to do what you need it to do. I have another series I call Avare, named after the city that Franciso is from. It's a mostly Turk cymbal that has a singular spiral in the center and a little bit of lathing on the edge. They are kind of silvery; drier, darker, a little funkier, but, again, versatile enough to use in a wide range. There is some other stuff in the works. I still do some stainless steel. I feel that stainless steel is a valid metal for cymbal making, but they can suck. I have found that the way to get a good sound with stainless steel is to make the cymbal large and thin- like up to 30". That is how you're going to get the low tone, and the body, and the musicality of bronze.

Lathing that stuff is very dangerous. If something hits you in the face, you're in trouble. I don't lathe steel to remove material. I will lathe steel for cosmetic reasons and I will lathe to put grooves in- it is mostly hammering, and a little bit of surface treatment.

For the bronze I use mainly (90%) Turkish blanks, I have bought Chinese blanks, I have used Brazilian bronze which is very very good bronze. It's all B-20 but there are subtle differences.

There are no bad cymbals. There may be some poorly made cymbals, but one of those cymbals may work for you. Choose cymbals for what it is that you need to play.

MORLANG PERCUSSION
Germany
https://morlangpercussion.de/

When I was fed up (and ears) with my first beginner cymbals on the drum set, I started looking for THE ideal cymbal set. Fast I had to realize that of course there is no such thing. But the search opened up the wonderful wide world of cymbal production and bronze processing for me. I began to read deeper and deeper into the matter and visited a traditional cymbal forge in Istanbul to experience the production of cymbals according to centuries-old craftsmanship up close. Influenced by these impressions, I tentatively started my first own attempts at bronze processing. I modified old used cymbals by hammering, adding rivets, or cutting out holes. These experiences quickly gave rise to the idea of producing hand-hammered bronze triangles, which after some experimentation to the triangles that I offer for sale today.

SILVIO MORGER
https://www.instagram.com/silviomorger

MUYSK
Colombia
Calle 72 #20 C-54 San Felipe neighborhood, Bogota, Colombia
https://www.muyskcymbals.com/   comercial@muyskcymbals.com

MUYSK was born in order to provide a solution to the lack of options and high prices that musicians had to assume when buying cymbals for their drums. This is because in Latin America we can only find brands of dishes imported from the United States and Europe.

This is how the first company dedicated to the manufacture of cymbals for drums, bands and orchestras was created, inspired by pre-Hispanic metallurgy as a point of reference, achieving the fusion between artisanal creation and the technical production of cymbals, to forge unique and versatile sounds. .

NEBULAE CYMBALS
Indonesia
https://www.nebulaecymbals.com/
nebulaecymbal@gmail.com

MATT NOLAN

https://www.mattnolancustomcymbals.com/

Matt Nolan is a British cymbalsmith and maker of other metal percussion instruments, many of them bespoke. Matt has created instruments for drummers, orchestras, composers, museums and galleries. Notable clients include Bjork, Danny Elfman, King Crimson, Massive Attack, Sebastian Rochford, Dame Evelyn Glennie, Mike Patton's Mondo Cane, Stella Artois, Louis Vuitton, Zappa Plays Zappa, Danish underwater art-music group "Between Music: Aquasonic", and German Turner Prize winning artist Wolfgang Tillmans. Matt's work has been displayed in galleries in London and New York, including MOMA, The Rubin Museum and Somerset House Many of the world's top Opera and Symphony Orchestras use Matt's instruments.

Matt has been a drummer since his early teens but followed an academic education and career path into the world of microelectronics and semiconductors – designing parts of silicon chips for digital TV and movie equipment, broadband wireless systems, and secure encryption, authoring a number of granted patents along the way.

Around 2005, the cymbal bug really started to bite and by the end of 2008, Matt had left the high tech world to combine his artistic and engineering sensibilities to start a one-man business making metal percussion instruments using just hands, ears and simple tools: off-the-shelf, customised or completely self-constructed.

Matt is self-taught, from tinkerer to hobbyist to professional. He started out mostly with cymbals and gongs – making them from pieces of or whole existing but broken cymbals, and with an eye for sculptural form. Shortly after that, he started more from scratch with industrial sheet metals of various alloys, and finally using the age-old tried and tested cymbal and gong alloys. Matt still employs a wide variety within the traditional metals – selecting blanks from Turkey, China, Germany or Japan depending on the specific sonic or working properties that best suit the desired musical outcome.

Under the brand "Matt Nolan Custom", he now produces other instruments, mostly for the orchestral world, including triangles, tubular bells (chimes), tuned gongs, bell plates and triangle beaters. Sound relaxation and therapy practitioners come to Matt for gongs and other resonating metals. Starting a few years ago, drummers and orchestral percussionists began to commission research projects for Matt to re-create favourite instruments that were either broken or saved only for special occasions, or unique but in reasonable demand for more of the same. This reverse engineering and experimentation to unlock the secrets of the original, long-gone artisans has led to replicas and homages mostly in the realms of triangles and cymbals (both jazz and orchestral), but also recreations of bygone instruments from Ancient Rome and Ancient Egypt for example.

Cymbals remain a favourite, and Matt believes there will always be more to learn, more to discover and more to master. There is an infinity of possibilities even in something as simple as a single piece of metal.

NUGIS
Russia

https://vk.com/nugiscymbals

Nugis Ivan Vladimirovich is the cymbalsmith behind Nugis Cymbals. Nugis translates to "marten", the furry creature that inhabits the northern hemisphere. Hence the logo. Ivan crafts his cymbals using traditional hand hammering methods in the town or Yugorsk City in Siberia...yes that Siberia. He's Russia's only cymbalsmith

OMETE CYMBALS
China

ometecymbals.com   kevin@ometecymbals.com   +86 151 6885 2837
Ji'Nan omete musical Instruments Co. Ltd

The company is located in Ji'nan city, Shandong Province, China. After 10 years of research and development, the company was finally established in November 2020. It is a factory specializing in the production of cymbals and gongs The company combines all the experience of the same occupation and and it is equipped with the most advanced equipment to make up for the shortcomings of the same industry for cymbals.There are various styles of cymbals of our customers can be cusomized by our professional masters, and a professional tuning team provides customers with various professional sound cymbals.We have hand-made cymbals, semi-manual and semi-mechanical cymbals, and fully automatic mechanical cymbals. The experience is very rich and varied. In order to better serve customers,The company adheres to the attitude of virtue, honesty, trust and harmony to provide customers with better convenience.

ORION CYMBALS
Brazil

Rua Monte Fuji, 290 Bairro dos Altos – Barueri – SP
CEP: 06423-030
https://orioncymbals.com.br/

OTTAVIANO
USA

https://www.instagram.com/ottavianocymbals
https://www.facebook.com/justin.ottaviano.1/
Justin Ottaviano

from *Drummers World*:   Justin Ottaviano makes his own cymbals. He uses the best quality Turkish blanks. The alloy is cast bronze B20, which is 80% copper and 20% tin. He makes all of the cymbals from the shaping process to the finishing of the logos. He shapes the cymbals profile, using a special technique that was shown to him by his family.

PGB Cymbals
Canada

https://www.pgbartisancymbals.com   https://www.instagram.com/pgb.artisancymbals/
Physical address: 5425 Rue de Bordeaux, Montréal QC H2H 2P9, Canada
Email: pgb.artisancymbals@gmail.com   Phone number: 4383941909

Philippe Gauthier Boudreau, combines traditional and modern techniques of hammering and lathing to offer you the desired sound, whatever the musical context.

PAISTE
Switzerland

Switzerland: Paiste AG Kantonsstrasse 2 CH-6207 Nottwil +41-41-939-3333
USA: Paiste America, Inc. 460 Atlas St. 92821 Brea, California Toll Free: +1-800-472-4783
Germany Paiste GmbH & Co. KG Gorch-Fock-Str. 13 D-24790 Schacht Audorf +49 4331 9479 0
https://www.paiste.com/

Garza
Paiste part 1

Readers are encouraged to learn more about Paiste by reading Hugo Pinksterboer's *The Cymbal Book* and listening to Dan Garza's two Youtube interviews with Bart van der Zee of The Drum History Podcast.

Garza
Paiste part 2

The details of Paiste's bronze production, from Patent Number: 4,809,581 Mar. 7, 1989

An alloy containing, for example, 14.7 percent by weight tin, 0.08 percent by weight phosphorus and 85.22 percent by weight copper is initially melted in an induction melting furnace. The melt is delivered at a temperature of 1000° C. to 1200' C. into a heat retention or holding furnace of a strip or band casting installation. A strip or band is cast. The caststrip or band has, for example, a width of 670 mm and a thickness of 18 mm. This strip or band cannot be coiled and is therefore cut into plates of approximately 3 to 4 meters length. Such plates are now homogenized at 600 C. to 700 C. during about 10 to 25 hours. Then the casting and oxidation skin is removed by means of a milling tool or cutter or equivalent structure. Thereafter the plates are initially only slightly cold rolled, i.e. by about 20 percent and then recrystallized at temperatures between 500 C. and 700 C. This process 10 15 20 25 30 35 45 50 55 65 4. cycle of cold rolling and recrystallization takes place until a final sheet or plate thickness of 1 to 2 mm is obtained. Then a final annealing is carried out at temperatures between 400 C. and 500 C. The obtained grain size then should be between 0.003 and 0.015 mm. The hardness should lie between 150 250 kiloponds per square millimeter, depending on the strived for sound or tone character. Now circular blanks or discs of, for example, 200 to 610 mm in diameter are cut out of this sheet or plate from which there is formed the aforedescribed cymbal 1. The cymbal 1 shown by way of example in FIG. 1 and described with reference thereto can be fabricated as follows: The dome or cup 11 is formed at the corresponding blank or disc heretofore described by pressing, die stamping, drawing or in any other suitable manner. The hole or aperture 111 is drilled into the zenith or apex of the dome or cup 11. Further forming or shaping is carried out by hammering the cold material. The thus formed or shaped cymbal is superficially faced or surface finished, preferably by hand, and then provided with a suitable conservation or preserving layer or film. In comparison with a traditional cymbal formed or shaped in analogous manner the inventive cymbal renders possible a totally new sound dimension.

MICHAEL PAISTE
HANDMADE CYMBALS & GONGS
Switzerland

https://www.facebook.com/michaelpaistecymbals/
https://www.instagram.com/michael.paiste
michael.paiste@gmail.com

PANTHEON PERCUSSION
office in Singapore, manufactured in Turkey
https://pantheonpercussion.com/

From the website:

We set our hearts on creating a Singaporean brand of B20 world-class cymbals that would be conceptualised in Singapore but handcrafted by our friends in Istanbul, Turkey. We wanted a Singaporean take on the famed Turkish cymbal: classic, musical, warm, powerful, pure, complex and durable. We also wanted the cymbals to reflect the Singaporean soul: modern, progressive, and harmonious. This marriage of timeless tradition with Singaporean innovation gave birth to Pantheon Percussion Cymbals. Our cymbals are cast bronze cymbals crafted from the best Turkish B20+ alloy. Our master craftsmen cast, temper, roll, cut, hammer, and lathe the cymbals with expert skill and a keen eye for attention. Only perfection can emerge from the foundry.

PERGAMON
TURKEY
https://www.pergamoncymbalsshop.com/en/sobre-pergamon-cymbals/

Pergamon Cymbals was founded by third generation masters, Saadettin KOÇ and Hakan FİDAN They have more than 50 years of experience combined making cymbals.

From the website:

THE ART OF DISH-FORGING is an ancient Anatolian (Asia Minor) craft that was perfected by Armenian masters since the beginning of the seventeenth century. It was developed during the Ottoman Empire and today, we are proud to preserve the same artisanal process that we have been developing for hundreds of years.

Traditional forging, and hand-produced, gives each Pergamon cymbal a unique sound. It requires highly experienced teachers who know perfectly the tradition and spirit of this musical instrument.

There is a long way to becoming a master craftsman. Fortunately, at Pergamon Cymbals we have third-generation teachers

S.P. PARKKINEN CYMBALS
Finland

Antti Sameli (Sami) Parkkinen Pehulantie 36   32740 Sastamala, Finland
tel. +358503446912
https://www.spparkkinencymbals.fi/en/   sparkn16@gmail.com

S.P. (Sami) started his cymbalmaking in 2022 under the tutelage of Dave Collingwood while also gathering knowledge and gaining skills from correspondence with some leading cymbalsmiths around the world and deriving inspiration from the history of this art. In his production, being a pre-60's drummer himself, Sami is leaning towards the tradition, especially the early fifties being close to his heart.

Hailing from a family with many artists and craftspeople and coming from a background of being a writer for over 30 years (novelist, playwright, translator) and a schooled plus graduated luthier (2016), Sami nowadays resides in Sastamala dividing his working hours between these various forms of art.

Before starting at this craft S.P. spent many years listening, playing, studying, buying and talking these beautiful instruments. He's continually in close contact with some top drummers and has the privilege to closely study and get inspired by their best instruments.

S.P.Parkkinen cymbals are Cafted from finest Turkish B20 bronze blanks. The bells are hand-forged except when mentioned otherwise.

Each cymbal is shipped FREE worldwide (exc. the taxes in Customer's country) plus each cymbal can be modified once during the first 3 moths after initial payment or traded to another S.P. Parkkinen cymbal of the same or smaller size witi no extra cost except shipping, or to a larger diameter one for a fee of 50 euros an inch.
Sami also modifies cymbals. Contact via email.

PUG CYMBALS
Australia

https://www.pugcymbals.com/

Based in Sydney Australia, drummer / educator James Waples has been forging his own path as a cymbalsmith under the branding PUG Cymbals since 2019. As an active musician he has performed and toured with Australian / international jazz greats for the past 20 years. James currently divides his time between PUG Cymbals and as the drummer for indie artist Donny Benét.

PUG Cymbals is focused on creating unique cymbals influenced by the great companies / independent cymbalsmiths of the past as well as exploring contemporary sounds for the future.

QUIJANO CYMBALS
Belgium
https://www.quijanocymbals.com/
fromthe website:

Quijano Cymbals is a small workshop located in Grimbergen, Belgium, ran solely by independent cymbalsmith Mariano Gabriel Quijano

There's something about the feeling you get once you hold an object handmade by yourself, be it artful, merely functional, or in the best case a combination of both. The feeling of creating something tangible, of crafting, the detailed nature of the process behind it; this has been the source from which I've gathered and keep on gathering to move forward, to get to where I am and where I will be.

I was born and raised in Caracas, Venezuela. Since childhood I've always seen myself involved in one form or another of creatively expressive activities. But it was music, specifically the drum-set, which rapidly took over and my adult life followed the path of a first aspiring, then professional jazz musician all throughout my 20's, which led me around the world.

During late 2019, I found myself yet again migrating somewhere new, this time towards Bogotá, Colombia. There coalesced the first steps of a goal I had given myself ten years prior: to someday be able to make a cymbal by myself, from start to end. I was hired to work at MUYSK, a small up and coming cymbal factory. They took a chance and brought me in with no previous experience. I outgrew myself at a fast pace. We did everything in the vein of Turkish tradition, from the crucible to the inking station. I started as a hired hand, hammering 6-8 hours at a time in a small room, lathing, pouring, tempering, cleaning and any other necessary tasks, 5 to 6 days a week. However, by the end of my stay with them I was helping with quality control, prototyping and re-writing some of the series' production processes. I hold for them an immense and profound sense of gratefulness; for sharing, for opening heavy doors, for allowing me to take my first steps into this now life project.

Today, after a lifetime of obsession and a deep love for cymbals, over a decade of working as a musician while envisioning and pursuing this here project, and my time at MUYSK; Quijano Cymbals is the materialization of a long-held aspiration with a trail of constant effort and heaps of work. My workshop is my dearest achievement, it is all I've physically got. What I create in there I do with the utmost respect and sense of responsibility, not only for my craft, but for those who helped me get here. I am nothing without them. I hope, if nothing else, that this shows through my work, conversely, allowing me to continue crafting, for nothing else other than the love of making.

QUIQEG
Italy
https://www.facebook.com/enrico.dalessandro.94

Bologna Italia Independent cymbal maker

For any contact follow me on Instagram at Quiqeg_cymbalsmith

Lives in Bentivoglio, Emilia-Romagna, Bologna, Italy

TIMOTHY ROBERTS

Timothy is a professional studio and live musician with 50+ album credits and extensive work as an on-call musician. His passion for sound exploration led him to crafting the instruments that he plays.

from Timothy's blog post "Cymbal Basics":

A cymbal is made up of a combination of metals that is shaped using heat, pressure, and stress. Different cymbal materials include brass, steel, b8 bronze, and b20 bronze to name a few. However, b20 bronze is the most common cymbal alloy for mid to high-end cymbals.

A cymbal makes a sound due to the tension that it's held in through the pressing, hammering, lathing, and burnishing processes. Think about how a guitar string is tensioned up. If you detune it, at a certain point it becomes limp and makes no sound. The tighter you tension it, the higher pitched it gets and at a certain point it will snap. Cymbal metal acts in a similar manner. Little to no tension equals little to no resonance and a low pitch. The more tension a cymbal has, the tighter the feel and the higher the pitch.

Then there is the thickness of the cymbal (determined by its weight) and the taper (where the thickness/weight is distributed). This aspect is hugely important as well. The thicker/heavier a cymbal is, the higher the pitch will be. Heavy, bright cymbals are loud and cut very well in a mix, but many drummers nowadays seek darker, more complex tones. Many vintage and high-end cymbals were designed to be thinner and more expressive. That doesn't necessarily mean that one is "better" than the other. It all comes down to preference and musical application.

The next aspect is the profile (or shape) of the cymbal. There is the bow, the cup (bell) size, and the circumference. They all affect the sound in various ways. Essentially the flatter the cymbal's bow, the lower the pitch, the darker, and the longer sustain will be. If the bow is more extreme (or "umbrella" shaped), the effect is a higher pitch and shorter sustain. The bell size affects the resonance of a cymbal (among other things). This is why flat rides (w/ no bell) tend to have a very short sustain. The bell allows the cymbal's pitch to ring out and the size/shape of the bell determines just how that pitch sounds and how it resonates. The circumference is one of the simplest aspects; the smaller the cymbal, the higher the pitch and vice versa.

These aspects (alloy, tension, thickness, taper, and profile) combine to create the overall sound of a cymbal. Every element affects every other and that is why cymbal-smithing is no easy task.

Big cymbal companies can produce thicker, machine-hammered cymbals for cheaper and with more consistency than they can produce hand-hammered cymbals. That distinction is evident in the cost and accessibility of "brighter" cymbals in today's market. That, combined with the advent of amplified instruments and louder music in the 70s and 80s, created the perfect environment for these kinds of cymbals to take center stage in the product catalogs of many big cymbal companies.

However, many drummers these days are looking for more expressive cymbals. That's partly why I started "Timothy Roberts Handcrafted Cymbals". I was consistently unsatisfied with the cymbals I purchased online, and I found that the sound in my head didn't exist.

https://reveriedrums.com/

(336) 701-5943

ROYAL CYMBALS
USA
info@royalcymbals.com

Note: See Paul Francis, page XX

RYET CYMBALS
India
https://ryetcymbals.com/

Ryet Cymbals was founded in 2022 by Shubham Bhardwaj in Jamshedpur, India. He began his journey as a cymbal smith after realizing the potential of his homeland to produce high-quality B20 cymbals considering their history with bell metal. The lack of any traditionally produced cymbals regionally was also a major contributing factor. Being a drummer himself and having no prior experience in metalworking, Shubham started teaching himself the art of cold-working metal with brass sheets and later with B20 cymbal blanks for over a year before his efforts bear fruit. Now, Ryet Cymbals crafts each instrument from start to finish by hand with the finest materials available in India. Operating in a small workshop in Jamshedpur, Ryet Cymbals hope to provide drummers in India with the highest quality cymbals at never seen before prices.

SABIAN
Canada
219 Main St.Meductic, NB, Canada E6H 2L5
Phone: 1-506-272-2019 1-506-272-2019 (local)
customerservice@sabian.com

SAGURTON, J David
USA
https://www.facebook.com/jdavid.sagurton

SALUDA CYMBALS
USA
(803) 446-8000 https://www.saludacymbals.com/ info@saludacymbals.com

We are the only true custom cymbal company around! With all the hype going around for custom drums, why not get a set of custom cymbals? We have a wide variety of cymbal series and plenty of customizing options. In most of our cymbal lines, you can tell us how you want the cymbals to sound. And in some of our cymbal lines, you can even tell us how you want them to look (as far as lathed striping)!

We only offer professional cymbals in B20 bronze alloy to give full, complex, lively and very versatile sounding cymbals. We offer some of the best sounding and most unique looking cymbals on the planet! You really get your money's worth. Our cymbals come to life on stage where you, your band mates and your viewing audience will hear and feel the difference. Cymbals are a part of music; Let them be heard! Let them be felt!

SAMSUN
Turkey
https://samsun-cymbals.com/

From the website:

Mustafa Diril, the founder, head and foreman of SAMSUN CYMBALS, started his apprenticeship at the young age of 17 at Istanbul Cymbals in 1988, where he learned the art of manufacturing cymbals from his foremen Mehmet Tamdeger and Agop Tomurcuk right down to the last detail. Then, in 1999, he made the decision to return to his hometown Samsun and to establish his own cymbal manufacture together with his cousins. Here, he significantly contributed to the development and the production of famous product lines for two of the leading and most popular cymbal brands in the world. In 2006, he founded his own cymbal brand SAMSUN Cymbals and started with only three employees in a very small manufacture to produce high-class, handmade cymbals.

BRUNO SCHELL

https://www.instagram.com/cymbalsbrunoschell

SCYMTEK
Office in USA, Production in Turkey
525 w allen ave , unit 13, San Dimas, CA 91773   909-596-5200
https://scymtek.com/

STEVE SEIFRIED
USA

https://www.facebook.com/steven.seifried/?locale=ms_MY&paipv=0&eav=Afa1WTuPmaFlR4swBT8ou-b2aVCMqfkZ2xNHNAu_7pJ5QwBlO84nxej5Rx3B7aep6T4Y&_rdr

SHELLEDY SOUNDS
USA
https://www.shelledysounds.com/

Brian Shelledy:
"Shelledy Sounds was conceived in 2011 when I began to make gongs from metals such as nickel-silver and different bronzes. I then built my own foundry, and began to offer cast instuments made from bell bronze."

SIHI
Office in Finland   Manufacturing in Turkey
Kroggårdsvägen 29 10300 Karjaa
https://www.sihicymbals.com/   info@sihicymbals.com

founder Ville Junttila

The idea of creating my own cymbals started developing little by little. It kept coming back again and again until I just had to do something about it! Finland does not have a strong tradition in cymbal making; actually, it does not exist.. So, where to go? Where all the iconic cymbals are being made in: Istanbul! After quite a lot of searching and talking with people in the industry, I found it! Perfectly what I was looking for: expert cymbal smiths with tons of experience and a massive passion for this project.

After lots of talking, going back and forth, and several days in a factory and, Sihi cymbals Cymbals were born! All Sihi Cymbals are made from scratch, as traditional, legendary Turkish cymbals are. Cast from high-quality bronze (known as B20), rolled, hammered, milled, finished, polished all by highly professional cymbal smiths. Sound is the main criteria. Cymbal smiths listen to the cymbals, and from there, decide when there has been enough hammering, and milling… So that's. That's why there are minor differences in the weights of the cymbals.

So, where does that name "Sihi" come from? Well, it was initially it was a joke and became the working title, and evidently, it stayed. But "Sihi"" comes from the Finnish word" "sihisee" – sizzles" – in English. It is also a slang word for brewed beverages, "Sihi-juoma."

SILKEN
China
https://kimus.n.nu/silken-cymbals

Wuhan-based SILKEN Cymbals was founded by master cymbalsmith, Ken Cheng in 2005. SILKEN specializes in B20 cymbals designed for modern applications. The cymbals are forged, lathed and hammered using centuries-old techniques, but have a very contemporary feel, comparable to offerings from major manufacturers.

JESSIE SIMPSON
Czech Republic
US Number +1 707.591.6318
Czech Number +420 737 284 797
https://www.jessesimpson.com/cymbals   jsjazz@gmail.com

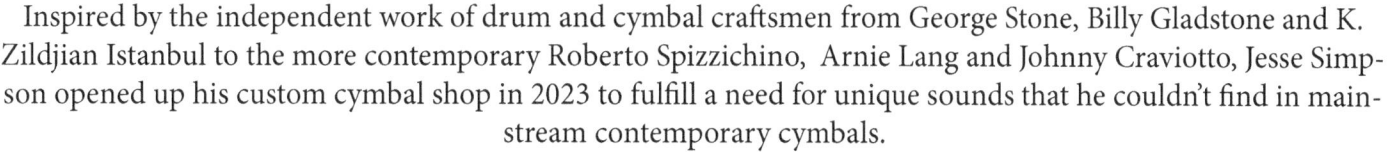

Inspired by the independent work of drum and cymbal craftsmen from George Stone, Billy Gladstone and K. Zildjian Istanbul to the more contemporary Roberto Spizzichino, Arnie Lang and Johnny Craviotto, Jesse Simpson opened up his custom cymbal shop in 2023 to fulfill a need for unique sounds that he couldn't find in mainstream contemporary cymbals.
Currently available original cymbals made from B20 blanks:

SKRETAS FAMILY CYMBAL COMPANY
USA
Manny and Caroline Skretas
New Braunfels, Texas
https://www.skretasfamilycymbals.com/
cymbalsalvage@gmail.com   210-749-8457

Based in New Braunfels, Texas, we are the only family owned and operated cymbal company in the state. We specialize in 100% hand crafted cymbals made from Turkish B20 bronze blanks, made for drummers of all genres. We look forward to meeting all of your cymbal needs

SMYRNA Cymbals
Turkey
www.symrnacymbals.com

(founded in 2008, location: Istanbul)

MOON BABY WALKING GONGS
USA
Jessie Snyder   https://gongs-unlimited.com/pages/moon-baby-walking-gongs
(402) 474-4664
Lincoln, NE 68507 USA

SOULTONE CYMBALS
Office USA, production in Turkey

Soultone Cymbals: https://www.soultonecymbals.com/ / https://www.soultonecymbals.de/ (company headquarters: USA; blanks by Masterwork)

SPECTRUM CYMBALS
USA
https://www.instagram.com/spectrumcymbals

Hand hammered, one of a kind cymbals made from B20 Bronze. These cymbals are made by hand in Fort Collins, Colorado by cymbalsmith David Lagueux

STAGG CYMBALS
Office in Belgium, manufactured in China
https://staggmusic.com/en

 The history of our brand goes back to Japan in the 1970s, where Stagg began life as a guitar company, creating a wide range of iconic models. In 1995, Leonardo Baldocci, the founder and chairman of renowned worldwide Belgian music distribution group EMD Music, relaunched and expanded the brand, with a mission to offer quality instruments, audio and lighting, and accessories at an affordable cost. Today, the Stagg brand is available in over seventy countries and has over 120 employees at its headquarters in Brussels, Belgium and around the world.
 On January 24th 2020, Stagg has celebrated its 25th anniversary, a sign of continuous growth and proven success in the global market. This is the perfect opportunity to celebrate our brand throughout the year.

SUPERNATURAL Cymbals
Office in USA, Made in Turkey
https://www.supernaturalcymbals.com/

Supernaturals Cymbals are traditionally crafted handmade B20 cymbals by the Salas and Okur families of Istanbul, Turkey and distributed in the USA by Willie Salas.

TONUM
Office in Ukraine, Made in Turkey

At this writing (2025), Website is down. Forums are full of complaints about this company having failed to provide any contact information and/or failing to deliver goods that have been paid for.

TONG XIANG

ZHANGQIU TONGXIANG MUSICAL INSTRUMENT FACTORY
Fanjia village, Shuizhai Township, Zhangqiu city, Shandong province
+86-531-83551048 / +86-13964138457
http://en.cncymbal.com   tongxiang200610@163.com

After People's Republic of China was founded in 1949, the first cymbal was born in Gong Factory of Zhoucun in Shandong Province, one of whose great founder was my ancestor.

.We are cymbal factory from China.
We can produce B25 B20 B8 BRASS and Alloy cymbals
If you like, we can also print your own logo on the cymbals.

T-CYMBALS
Turkey

Office: Ayazma Deresi Cad. Saral İş Merkezi Kat: 5/6-C, 34394
Beşiktaş / İstanbul - TURKEY
Showroom: Maslak Atatürk Oto San. 2. Kısım 27. Sok. No: 1092, 34398
Maslak / İstanbul - TURKEY
t. +90 (212) 286 10 88 m. +90 (533) 632 26 00
https://tcymbals.com   info@tcymbals.com

Dear one & all

After being involved in cymbal business as a marketing manager (agop cymbals & several Turkish cymbal companies) product specialist & cymbal designer for many years, I have formed my cymbal company T-Cymbals with a childhood musician friend of mine Mr. Burak Kulaksızoglu. Creating our own cymbals was a long time dream of ours, and we feel gifted now.

As a drummer/musician, we asked ourselves " Why we do it and why did we start making custom cymbals?" The answer is simple " We love cymbals ".

T-cymbal is the first musician owned cymbal company in the world. Our goal is to offer a product that is reliable, better built than the competitor's and give artists and customers the kind of treatment you would give to your family or close friends.

T-Cymbals is not another Turkish cymbal company; T-cymbals are as individual as you are, and like no other you have heard or seen before. We believe that you will see what we have going here is a special blend of quality, integrity and style.

Please kindly check our website at www.tcymbals.com

Arbak R. Dal

TRX Cymbals
Office in USA, production in Turkey
https://trxcymbals.com   sales@trxcymbals.com   (818) 751-3257

Production

TRAKIAN
Turkey
ARSLAN METAL SANAYİ VE TİCARET A.Ş
Kerimbey OSB, Sakarya Cd. NO:7/1, 55300 Tekkeköy/Samsun, Türkiye

Trakian Cymbals is an addition to Arslan Metal which has been a trusted name in the metal industry since 1964, providing the highest quality of Copper and Bronze products throughout Turkey. Over the years, they've built a reputation for excellence and environmental responsibility, with all business processes aimed at maintaining the highest level of integrity, quality, and cost competitiveness.

Over the last 60 years, Arslan Metal has developed a very high level understanding of chemical and physical metallurgy. By combining advanced metal technology with centuries-old cymbal-making techniques, Trakian Cymbals was born in 2021. Furthermore, because Arslan Metal manufactures such high volume industrial parts, they are able to offer their cymbals at an extremely competitive price.

Trakian is now becoming a premier Turkish cymbal manufacturer known for crafting high-quality, hand-hammered cymbals designed to meet the needs of drummers across all genres. With a deep respect for the Turkish tradition of cymbal-making methods, each Trakian cymbal is a work of art.

Production

TREXIST
Turkey

https://trexistcymbalsusa.com   info@trexistcymbalsusa.com
USA office: 5202 w Jupiter way N Chandler AZ 85226   +1 (786) 427 46 34

The Turkish Cymbal Manufacturing technique has been in music industry over hundreds of years and the formula is still kept in secret. The Trexist Cymbals Company was established inn April 2010 in Istanbul Turkey and has been operating its own factory by Dogukan Okur; the former CEO of Supernatural Cymbals. Since 2019, the head office is in Chandler, Arizona. Cymbals are shipped worldwide from there. We are a respectful traditional handmade Turkish cymbal company, but we are not limited by tradition. The Past had already been built. We use tradition to help build the future. We are always seeking new ideas for drummers or how to make our Cymbals better.

TRINITY CYMBALS
China
https://trinitycymbals.com/

The cymbals continue to be handcrafted, while the manufacturing continues to use modern quality controls to make the cymbals sound brilliant and resilient. Cymbals have been hand made and hammered in China for over 1000 years. Our cymbals have been handcrafted since 1949, by artisans who have learned from ancestors over many years. Located in the Shandong Province of China, our Cymbal-Smiths focus on old-world craftsmanship, integrity, and quality. These are traditionally cast cymbals made with the highest quality alloy metal which makes a unique sound that sets Trinity apart.

TUNYO
Poland
https://www.facebook.com/people/Tunyo-Handmade-Cymbals/100057479797749

TURCO
Turkey
Kavaklı Sok. No: 6, Orhanlı, 34956 Tuzla İstanbul
+90 545 138 10 11   https://turcocymbals.com   info@turcocymbals.com
Instagram: @turco.cymbals

TURKISH
Turkey
https://turkishcymbals.com   orkestra@turkishcymbals.com
Galip Dede Cad. No:55 A Beyoğlu / Istanbul / Turkey   +90 212 292 18 86
USA: https://www.turkishcymbals.us   info@turkishcymbals.us

From an online forum:

"Turkish Cymbals" was founded in 1996 in Istanbul by Mehmet Tamdeğer. He worked in Istanbul – Samatya with the Zildjian family and learned all the details and tricks of cymbal manufacture. Currently, he is the only craftsman alive, who worked with the Zildjian family and knows the techniques of handmade cymbal manufacture. After the Zildjian family immigrated to the USA and started manufacturing cymbals using machines, Mehmet Tamdeğer decided to continue manufacturing handmade cymbals in Turkey. First, he founded his own company called "Istanbul Mehmet Cymbals" and later he helped during the foundation of the company "Turkish Cymbals" on a partner's interest. All the craftsmen and artisans of the factory were trained by Mehmet Tamdeğer and he is still the latest person to finalize the manufacturing process by checking and confirming the cymbals.

UFIP
Italy
Via Galileo Galilei, 20 - 51100 Pistoia - Italy | Tel.: +39.0573.532066
https://www.ufip.it/
Kelley Distribution Group 240 N Dixie Highway #20 Hollywood, FL 33020
kelleydistribution.com 954 465-3946   david@kelleydistribution.com

VCYMBALS
TURKEY
https://vcymbals.com mail@vcymbals.com

Idea and Sound

Vintage Classic Cymbals are designed and founded by cymbal specialist and enthusiast, Torab Majlesi. Torab has worked as production manager/designer with various Turkish cymbals companies since 1997 and as a professional band/session drummer since 1990.

He started collecting and playing original Zildjian and Istanbul brand cymbals at an early age. His first cymbals were an old K set with a 22"ride, a pair of 13"hihat's, a 15"crash and a 12"splash which he played with a vintage Ludwig super classic maple bebop kit with an 18"bass,12"tom, and a 14" floor tom.

He bought those cymbals for 350 dollars (if you were to buy them now you would have to add another zero) in 1989 when he was 15 years old from a small music shop in Istanbul. (Unfortunately that set was stolen in 1994).

After years of research and development experience, playing and knowledge he acquired he developed his "1 Model-1 Cymbal" idea. Now there are dozens of cymbal companies worldwide with hundreds of models, but drummers are still searching for that old sweet cymbal and Vintage Classic Cymbals are that sound.

The main idea behind the design is making a cymbal with that great vintage look which produces a great classic sound that also can be played in any kind of music with an average volume and touch with little effort.

Brush and hand cymbal playing techniques are also a very important part of drums and percussion playing and Vintage Classic Cymbals works perfectly in these situations because of their sensitivity and response to the softest of strokes.

All of our cymbals are produced with the highest quality B25 bronze alloy composition which contains 25% tin, (the standard B20 has 20% of tin but Vintage

Classic Cymbals composition has 5% more of tin), to get that classic old K sound.

After the main production techniques of casting, lathing, and hammering are completed all of the cymbals go through an inspection process by Torab. He plays and checks them for perfection to determine that there are no defects, balance problems or un-wanted overtones. The cymbals then go through a and aging process which takes that great look and that nice dry sound that is experienced Classic Cymbals.

PRODUCTION

VANSIR Cymbals
China
Xifan Economic Development Area, Zhangqui District, Jinan City, Shandong Province
+86-531-83551597 https://www.vansircymbals.com info@vansircymbals.com

WHO WE ARE

Zhangqiu XuSheng Musical Instrument Factory is a family specializing in the production of brass percussion instruments.

Since my great-grandfather made bronze musical instruments in the Qing Dynasty, it has gone through three dynasties. We are the oldest bronze percussion instruments manufacturer in China and have a long history of manufacturing processes.

As time proceeds, we have combined the traditional hand made with the advanced production facilities to develop excellent manufacturing processes. With new formulas researching in recent ten years, we have created high-class goods, so that you have an extraordinary musical experience.

In our continuous improvement and innovation, we have developed products suitable for different music styles. They all have good expression and high music quality, to lead you into the real music hall.

JULIAN VLEMINKX
Belgium
https://belcymbalboutique.com/

WUHAN
office in USA, production in China
https://www.wuhancymbals.com sales@cardinalpercussion.com
Cardinal Percussion 1690 A Tibbetts Wick Road Girard, Ohio 44420
330-707-4446
sales@cardinalpercussion.com

XILXO
Office in USA, production in Turkey
https://cymbalhouse.com cymbalhouse@gmail.com
524 Main Street, Covington, KY 41011 (859) 866 9078

ZARRAS CYMBALS
USA
https://www.instagram.com/zarrascymbals/#

ZILDJIAN
USA
https://zildjian.com/
22 Longwater Drive, Norwell, MA 02061 781-871-2200

ZILLI CYMBALS
Office in Austria, manufacturing in Turkey
https://zillicymbals.com info@zillicymbals.com
Aydin 0430 609 162   Paul 0408 877 769

ZULTAN CYMBALS
Office in Germany, manufacturing in Turkey
https://www.zultancymbals.com

The Zultan Cymbal company was found in 2000 by Martin Hofmann of Musik-Service Aschaffenburg that was bought by Thomann GmbH in 2011. It's the housebrand of Thomann Music
Zultan uses B25 in the CS Series, the rest are B20.

REBEATS PUBLICATIONS

The Leedy Way
by Rob Cook
Leedy book & biography of George Way with sections on Camco, Conn, Advance, L&S

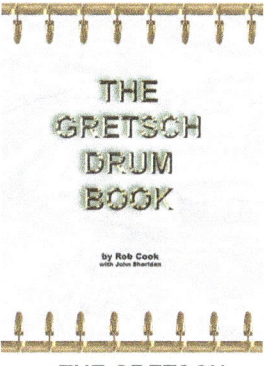
THE GRETSCH DRUM BOOK
by Rob Cook
with John Sheridan

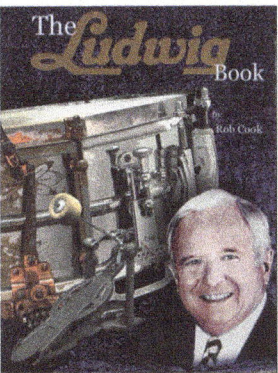
THE LUDWIG BOOK
by Rob Cook

THE SLINGERLAND BOOK
3rd Edition, by Rob Cook

THE ROGERS BOOK
by Rob Cook

Leedy Drum Topics

Franks For The Memories
Franks Drum Shop history

THE MAKING OF A DRUM COMPANY
by Wm F. Ludwig II

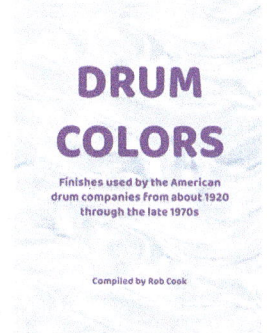
DRUM COLORS
by Rob Cook

REBEATS CALFSKIN HEAD BOOK
by Rob Cook

A History of Drums Made In Germany
by Fritz Steger

Gretsch Serial Number Dating Guide
by Rick Gier

Ludwig Serial Number Dating Guide
by Rick Gier

My Life In Percussion
by Karl Dustman

George Way's Little Black Book

Best Seat In The House
by Jerry Shirley

The Life & Times of Gene Krupa
by Bruce Crowther

1941 Gretsch catalog reprint

Hal Blaine And The Wrecking Crew
autobiography

Lucky Drummer
by Ed Shaughnessy
autpbiography

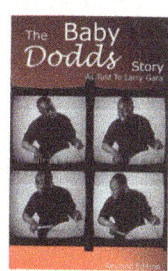
The Baby Dodds Story,
by Larry Gara

More info, prices, ordering info:

Rebeats.com   rob@rebeats.com   989-463-4757

www.ingramcontent.com/pod-product-compliance
Lightning Source LLC
Chambersburg PA
CBHW061128070526
44584CB00033B/4251